café life
LONDON

An Insider's Guide to the City's Neighbourhood Cafés

By Jennie Milsom

Photography by Hannah Moushabeck

and Harry Hall

Armchair Traveller
at the bookHaus

Published in the UK in 2012 by
The Armchair Traveller
at the BookHaus
70 Cadogan Place
London SW1X 9AH
www.thearmchairtraveller.com

Text copyright ©Jennie Milsom. 2012
Photography copyright © Hannah Moushabeck, 2012
(all except for ones listed below)
Photography copyright (Front cover. 2, 6, 16, 17, 18, 19, 21, 22, 23, 32, 42, 43, 44, 45, 46, 48, 49,
57, 58, 77, 78, 79, 81, 82, 87, 88, 91, 102, 103, 105, 131, 132, 133, 135, 136, 137, 138, 139, 149, 151, 154, 155,
156, 157, 158, 162, 163, 164, 165, 166, 167, 168.) ©Harry Hall, 2012
Photos on pages 52, 52, 54, 55 are courtesy of Orange Pekoe
Photos on pages 117, 119 are courtesy of Munson's

Design copyright ©Interlink Publishing, 2012
Map design by Julian Ramirez
Book design by James McDonald/The Impress Group
Published in agreement with Interlink Publishing

ISBN 978-1-907973-25-3
A CIP catalogue for this book is available from the British Library

Printed and bound in China

Contents

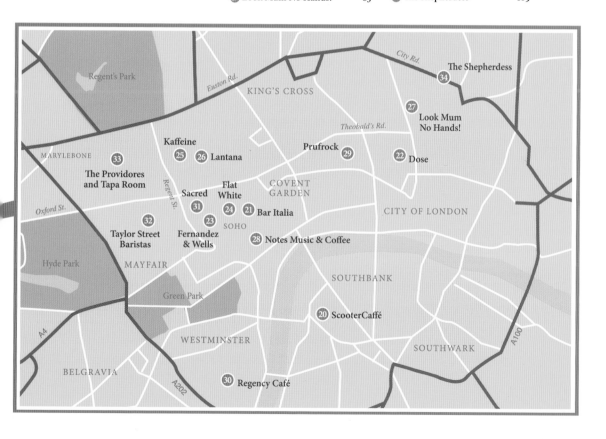

INTRODUCTION

C AFÉS HAVE BECOME A WAY OF LIFE in London. People can always seem to find some loose change for a mid-morning coffee and heading out for a sandwich at lunchtime is more flexible and affordable than a restaurant reservation. Serving a range of food from dawn until dusk, cafés offer convenient solutions for our busy lifestyles. And with pubs closing their doors up and down the country, it's possible that cafés are responding to a shift away from British drinking culture.

Café Life London was created by scouring every corner of the capital in the hope that a lead or a hunch might reveal a unique café around the corner. The result is a collection of 34 independent cafés whose owners tell their stories about the inspiration behind their ventures and what makes them stand out from the crowd. They share their tales of the slog and sacrifice that went into creating the café that's known and loved by its many customers.

Cafés take many forms and this book offers a range that's organised by café type throughout London's neighbourhoods. The first chapter is for coffee lovers. Offering more than a caffeine-fix, these are places where the coffee is made by a skilled barista who'll ensure that the coffee tastes great every time.

Despite the recent wave in specialty coffee, tea remains the nation's favourite drink and you'll discover where to savour the perfect brew, from a reliable English breakfast to truly original blends and infusions.

The traditional London "caff" is celebrated here, too. Many of these wonderful establishments have disappeared from London's streets. Their glorious interiors boasting Formica-topped tables, tiled walls and fixed seating remain largely untouched since their 1950s heyday. They offer a glimpse into years gone by and continue to dish up home-cooked food with a smile— a winning combination that cheers and satisfies.

And where would the residents of any city be without their neighbourhood café? Tucked away in residential backwaters and in central London's streets, these bolt-holes enrich the lives of many within their local community.

Finally, there are the cafés that you'll find hidden within other shops and outlets. Providing a chance to refuel and relax while shopping, these cafés are a harmonious marriage of elements that thrive and complement each other.

Whether they're known for their excellent coffee, intimate setting, or knock-out breakfasts, the magic ingredient behind all these cafés is the same: the people who have realized a vision through hard work and determination to create a special place for us all to enjoy.

Café culture is not a modern phenomenon. The City of London grew from the seventeenth- and eighteenth-century coffeehouses that were frequented by everyone from artists and writers to philosophers and politicians. Commoners and professionals united with like-minded peers they might not otherwise have met. News was exchanged, issues were debated and business was carried out over coffee. One of the most important institutions in the financial City, The London Stock Exchange, grew out of the coffeehouses—notably Jonathan's Coffee House in Change Alley—where stock-brokers first started to buy and sell shares.

By the early 1900s the coffeehouse era had dwindled and coffee-drinking gave way to tea. Inspired by the flamboyant pavement cafés in Paris with their tables spilling out onto the wide boulevards, a café society started to emerge in London. These cafés were stomping grounds for artistic circles and frequented by artists, poets and writers who could come together and be inspired.

Coffee later found its way into people's homes in the form of freeze-dried instant. Made in seconds by mixing with hot water, it was readily available and enjoyed for its convenience. It is still the most widely consumed type of coffee in Britain—the average consumer is four times more likely to turn to instant coffee than freshly ground.

The post-war 1950s celebrated a new type of café with a new type of coffee—espresso. This strong, dark liquid was brewed from ground coffee in espresso machines whose milk-steamers transformed it into frothy cappuccinos. Italian-owned Moka Bar in Soho's Frith Street was credited as being the first espresso bar in London when it opened in 1953. It was a hit with the local Italian community and music-loving teenagers who were too young to drink in pubs.

Fast-forward four decades and coffeehouse chains started to take root in London, becoming big business. Suddenly London was awash with skinny lattés and coffee-themed merchandise as these roaster-retailers from Starbucks to Costa Coffee romanced customers with soothing music and comfy sofas.

After the First Wave of instant coffee and the Second Wave of coffeehouse chains, the twenty-first century brought a new appreciation of coffee. This Third Wave focusses on ethically sourcing quality coffee from single estates, fostering relationships with coffee farmers and showcasing the potential of these magical beans.

With comfort high on the agenda—sitting-in is becoming more popular than takeout—café customers are made to feel more at home than ever with newspapers, WiFi and loyalty cards. Yet there is no magic formula for creating atmosphere and it's hard to put a finger on the intangible qualities that make us prefer one café to another. Cafés, coffee shops, espresso bars—whatever they're called, *Café Life London* celebrates these social hubs where friends and family come together and where strangers mingle. Advice is shared, ideas flourish, and numbers are swapped.

Reminiscent of the coffeehouses 300 years ago, it seems London's café culture has come full circle. Work your way through the cafés in this book while sampling some amazing food and drink along the way and you'll discover another side to London. Whatever you're looking for in a café, you'll find it here in *Café Life London*.

· 1 ·

COFFEE

THERE IS NO DOUBT that London has become serious about its coffee. In recent years, independent cafés and coffee shops have sprung up in central London shopping districts and in far-flung neighbourhoods. Smaller-scale coffee roasters, such as East London-based Square Mile, have become something of a stamp of quality on a coffee shop's menu.

We've progressed from instant coffee to the fancy lattés offered by high-street chains and beyond to what's become known as the Third Wave of coffee—artisan coffee shops and brew bars that focus on serving traceable coffee made with precision and skill. That's not to say that British high streets are no longer dominated by chains. Gradually, though, we are becoming more aware of what constitutes a well-made coffee and are more likely to go out of our way to find one.

For the serious coffee drinker the provenance of the coffee beans and the links with the coffee farmer have become more pertinent than gimmicky terms and labelling. Whereas previously baristas were perfecting their milk-steaming techniques, the focus has returned to the flavour of the coffee and to extracting the cleanest, roundest flavours from these beans. It's hardly surprising that filter coffee has started to nudge milky espresso-based lattés and cappuccinos off the bar. Without milk to hide behind, suddenly the brew itself is the star. And yet for some, the methods of producing a decent coffee—be it espresso or filter—range from the particular to downright obsessive. The beans are ground to the nearest fraction of a gram, the temperature of the water measured to the nth degree and the extraction meticulously timed.

The history of coffee in London began in the old coffeehouses with the first one opening in 1652 in the City of London. Coffeehouses were social centres where business was carried out

by men (women were banned) who could talk finance, art and politics. They were places to philosophize, write, and entertain. Coffeehouses soon sprung up on every street corner and in the eighteenth century they became known as Penny Universities because of the penny charged to enter. Intelligent, educating conversation was fuelled by caffeine, the magical drug that restored alertness. Coffee was the thinking-man's alternative to gin and beer that was consumed in vast quantities in London's bawdy bars and alehouses.

Coffee might no longer cost a penny a cup but, in some respects today's cafés that are celebrated for their well-crafted coffee are not dissimilar to the coffeehouses of the seventeenth and eighteenth Centuries. Visit any of the cafés that follow and you can be sure that the money you hand over for your dark brew will be worth every penny and the detour.

Prufrock Coffee

23-25 Leather Lane, Clerkenwell EC1N 7TE
020 7404 3597 www.prufrockcoffee.com
Open: 8AM-6PM Mon to Fri,
10AM-4.30PM Sat, 11AM-4PM Sun
Tube/rail: Chancery Lane, Farringdon

"THE IDEA of making delicious coffee is pretty new," says former World Barista Champion Gwilym Davies who co-owns Prufrock Coffee. "We're exploring, learning and sharing that information. We're just giving people a nice experience."

In March 2011 Gwilym teamed up with fellow barista Jeremy Challender and German baker Klaus Kuhnke to open Prufrock Coffee in Leather Lane. It's a coffee-shop that focusses on quality espresso and brewed coffee. You can sit at the bar and be dazzled by coffee brewing theatrics or settle down at one of the tables dotted around the room and enjoy a well-made latté, a slice of cake, and the soothing sound of classic jazz. In the basement there's a training centre where professional and home baristas can perfect latté art, sample coffees, and test-drive espresso machines.

The people behind Prufrock are the movers and shakers of coffee's Third Wave, a celebration of coffee that's committed to ethically sourced, quality coffee from bean to cup. "We want to know the farm the beans are from, the harvest dates, the processing method . . . All this affects the way we'll use them," says Gwilym. Every morning the baristas set up the bar for the day. During this "dialling in" process, they tweak timings, temperatures and weights. They taste the coffees and get a feel for

the best brewing method. Extracting the natural sweetness that's locked within the coffee beans is the ultimate aim and it's quite a skill. "Under-extracted is sour and over-extracted is bitter. Somewhere in the middle is the sweetness," says Jeremy, who you'll often find behind the bar.

Prufrock on Leather Lane was opened as a response to the interest in coffee at Gwilym's coffee-carts in East London and the first outlet of Prufrock—a coffee-bar that he and Jeremy set up and ran with another barista champion from Sweden in a menswear boutique on Shoreditch High Street. Both ventures were conduits for honing barista skills, educating customers about coffee, and lapping up feedback. "We had customers behind the counter so many times, explaining to them about coffee," says Gwilym. "We realized there was a huge demand for training. We wanted to explore not just espresso but different ways of brewing."

Gwilym never set out to win the World Barista Championship—he entered to improve his coffee-making skills—but when he won, he became an ambassador for the UK's coffee scene. Instead of dragging his coffee-carts out in the wind and rain five days a week, he travelled the world from Kenya to Moscow, visiting coffee growers and speaking at events. Today he continues to train baristas and give talks overseas for friends and contacts he's established since his 2009 win.

At Prufrock Coffee the L-shaped counter is two-fold. One part is given over to a shiny Nuova Simonelli espresso machine from where you can order "espresso with milk" in 4oz, 6oz, or 8oz cups. It's a simplified coffee menu without the conventional name-tags. And then there's the brew-bar where you can pull up a stool and watch a barista brew your coffee by all manner of techniques from filter to siphon.

To the untrained eye the brew bar resembles a new-age laboratory though Jeremy dismisses it as being more Year Seven "pseudo" science. First there's the streamlined boiler, a gleaming water dispenser that's integrated into the countertop and produces hot water to the nearest tenth of a degree at the touch of a button. It doubles as a drip-tray and a scale for the water to be weighed according to the brewing recipe. "It does everything," says Jeremy. "It probably even does toast." Then there are siphons—age-old brewers with a hi-tech overhaul—that are clamped above the orange glow of Japanese beam heaters. "The siphon is a cleaner way of making coffee. It's a short extraction, a stable temperature and makes a refined cup," he explains. "To bring more body to the coffee, we'd brew in a wood-neck because the cloth filter lets some oils through."

This is about more than merely sipping the end result. It's a one-to-one with a coffee expert who will guide you through details about the coffee's origin, brewing technicalities and tasting notes. Most of the coffees come from East London's Square Mile Coffee Roasters ("we know and trust them," says Gwilym) and Prufrock showcases beans from guest roasters around the world that Gwilym collects on his travels. And there are beans that simply find their way to Prufrock. "Things just turn up in this place," smiles Jeremy.

Staff are young, tattooed baristas in lace-up flats or Converse. Don't be fooled by their laid-back disposition. Their interest in coffee goes way beyond casual curiosity. Many compete in brewing contests and they live and breathe coffee. Jeremy recognises the advantage of having a competitive edge to the coffee scene. "It gets everyone together and there's a strong element of education. It's a healthy thing, it gives coffee a new audience." Everyone who works at Prufrock seems to have turned up from hanging around the coffee machines. "They're creative types and students, not necessarily from the coffee world but they enjoy food and flavours," says Gwilym. "We pulled them in because they had an interest." Jeremy, who is a trained pianist and teaches the piano, agrees. "There's an alliance with the arts world," he says. "Baristas often have links as painters, designers and musicians and they work in the coffee industry for a regular income."

And because Prufrock is as much a place for coffee-enthusiasts to refine their skills, the team is complemented by visiting baristas from around the world who work behind the bar. Like moths to a flame, they're drawn by Prufrock's reputation in the coffee world and the opportunity of being at the forefront of the evolving coffee scene in the UK.

Leather Lane was chosen as the site because it was a bit of a thoroughfare though Prufrock has become a destination in itself. It's a roomy, minimal space—a former sex-shop—with painted brick walls and pink-painted pillars. A hefty extraction duct and neat rows of glowing spotlights decorate the corrugated metal ceiling and coffee paraphernalia is displayed on bookcases around the room. A visual summary of the coffee being served is represented by bags of beans attached to lengths of coloured string that lead to examples of brewing methods and countries of origin on a world map.

On the edge of the financial City and not quite West End, Leather Lane is known for its food outlets and market stalls with their discount clothing, non-leather goods, and mobile phone accessories. Prufrock customers are a mix of professionals and locals who tap away on laptops and coffee-crazed day-trippers who make a pilgrimage to the brew-bar.

If you're after a panini or somewhere to chill out with the papers for the afternoon you're probably in the wrong place. Go to Prufrock for a caffeine-fix of the highest order and come away knowing more about coffee than you did before you set foot through the door. "This is not a finished concept," says Gwilym. "We want to keep pushing forward and bringing customers with us. Pushing relationships is the only way we can get better and learn from each other."

Dose

70 Long Lane, EC1A 9EJ
020 7600 0382 www.dose-espresso.com
Open: 7AM-5PM Mon to Fri, 9AM-4PM Sat
Tube/rail: Barbican, Farringdon, St Paul's,
City Thameslink

DOSE'S OWNER, James Phillips, describes his coffee as artisan. "I set out to master a craft, much like a carpenter, jeweller or baker, to meld science and art. It's about doing the best you can with what you've got," he says. When it comes to sourcing beans, he chooses coffee roasters, such as East London's Square Mile and Staffordshire-based Has Bean, whose beans are traded ethically and often directly with the coffee farmers. "I am the last in a long line of artisans—farmers, pickers, sorters and roasters—and my job is to make sure that all these people's hard work is exemplified as best as I can," James says. With his meticulous attention to detail—from ethical sourcing to brilliant extractions—James is recognized as one of the country's top baristas and has successfully competed at the national level in the UK Barista, Aeropress, and Brewer's Cup Championships.

Social networking means James is constantly in touch with a whole bunch of people he'd never normally have met. He offers guest coffees from roasters in the UK, Scandinavia, and the United States that he tracks down in web shops or from people he meets on coffee forums. For him, though, the key criteria is always whether the beans have been ethically traded and he

believes it's more complex than simply being labelled Fairtrade. "Fairtrade, like other badges that started with good intentions, is beginning to be hijacked by the big boys and exploited, along with the farmers, for profit. It says nothing about the quality," he says, "only that a 'fair' price was paid. Direct Trade, however, often fosters a quality-minded approach, as the buyer and coffee producer can communicate directly with each other. It empowers the coffee growers as they can negotiate a better price for better coffee."

You'll usually find James behind the counter in Dose on Long Lane, moments from Smithfield Meat Market, one of the oldest markets in London. Dose is an espresso bar that focusses on consistently excellent coffee and offers a range of simple food, such as freshly made sandwiches, pastries and bakes. The café started life at 69 Long Lane. Anticipating an increase in footfall from Farringdon station's redeveloped entrance and ticket hall across the road, James shifted his café into the larger space next-door in May 2011.

Along with espresso-based coffees, Dose also offers filter-style Aeropress and Clever Dripper. "They're the best for space and speed," James says. He's constantly tweaking the variables of the coffee such as the grind and the temperature and experiments with brews and blends including fine-tuning a slow-brew coffee that drips through the night and is served cold. "Latté art is less important to me than you might think," he says. "It's the cherry on the top, like dressing something up. If the texture and taste don't back it up, it's pointless." For every coffee sold, James donates one penny to Coffee Kids, a non-profit organization that aims to improve the lives of coffee-farming families. "For me it's a more direct way of making a contribution," he says. "I make money from coffee that is grown by some of the world's poorest people and I feel I have an obligation to give a little of that back."

Before making London his home, James trained as a chef in Wellington, New Zealand, and went on to work in the banking industry in Sydney, Australia. "It wasn't the life I wanted. It was soul-sapping," he says. He was fired—"it was inevitable"—and took a job in a café, a shoebox of a place in Sydney's King's Cross district where he was fortunate to work with a barista whose passion was "infectious". Still in Sydney, he worked for coffeehouse and roasters Toby's Estate and became friends with the owners. And so his love for coffee began. "I was nosying about, asking questions, soaking it all up," he says.

In 2006 he and his girlfriend (now wife) Helen moved to London and immediately spotted a gap in the market for decent coffee. It was an exciting time for coffee lovers in London—in Soho,

Sacred and Flat White cafés had recently opened, introducing London to an Antipodean-style of coffee. Although keen to start his own venture, James managed a restaurant during the week. On Saturdays he ran a coffee stall on Broadway Market which gave him the opportunity to meet coffee insiders and do some essential ground work in preparation for opening his own place.

James had never been to the Smithfield area but was attracted to the site on Long Lane because of the high volume of City workers. He took over the lease for number 69 in December 2008. "It was a horrible little greasy spoon café," he remembers. "I gutted the place and started again." In some respects, the site's miniscule dimensions worked in his favour as there was only one way a fridge or an espresso machine could go. He called it Dose because the name was snappy and he liked its medicinal connotation.

The current site at number 70 is by no means huge but much thought has gone into creating its striking interior. A red stripe runs diagonally across the ceiling connecting the door to the back window, cleverly guiding your eye across the counter. The red theme extends through to the shiny La Marzocco espresso machine and the crockery. Even the fire extinguisher and alarm on the wall comply with the colour scheme. The café offers more seating than the previous site at two restaurant-sized tables that James had custom-made for the café. Coffees of the week are chalked up on the blackboard and the drinks menu is spelt out on the wall with bright magnetic letters.

This isn't exactly mother-and-baby territory with its City postcode. The wooden floor in Dose is trod by well-heeled customers, mostly suited and booted, who scoot in for their early morning caffeine hit on the way to their desks or pause over a mid-morning coffee and catch-up with a colleague. The pace is fast and frantic but this doesn't seem to faze the average punter. About 70 percent of the coffee is takeout but if you time it right, you could slip into a seat and leaf through the paper or balance a laptop on your knee. Or, if the weather's fine, perch on a stool outside on the pavement with your coffee and watch the black cabs buzz by.

James's small team of baristas all have a hand in preparing the food. He recruits through on-line forums, seeking people who have at least an interest in coffee and are willing to learn. Most people he takes on already know each other through London's coffee scene. "Usually there are two degrees of separation," he says.

Flat White

17 Berwick Street, Soho W1F 0PT
020 7734 0370 www.flatwhitecafe.com
Open: 8AM-7PM Mon to Fri, 9AM-6PM Sat & Sun
Tube/rail: Oxford Circus, Piccadilly Circus,
Tottenham Court Road

FLAT WHITE IS THE SMALL SOHO CAFE with a huge reputation. Known to many of its loyal following and contemporaries as the granddaddy of coffee, this is the London caffeine den that's often credited with kick-starting the wave of Antipodean-style coffee bars in the UK. Today its dedicated team of baristas produces around 700 coffees every day.

In 2005 London had reached something of a plateau as far as the coffee scene was concerned. Italian cafés and sandwich bars still served strong cappuccinos and the branded American chains were pumping out their take on coffee by the bucket-load. Then New Zealander Cameron McClure arrived on the scene. Coffee had always been more than a hobby to him—he'd been making it since he left high school and had a professional set-up at home. He still remembers the first good coffee he had when he was just 16. It was a flat white, made by a barista called Tonto in his hometown Christchurch. It was something of a revelation for him. "I realized there was a major difference between coffee and serious coffee," Cam says. He went on to work in cafés in Christchurch while he was a student, fine-tuning his barista skills.

With his Scottish ancestry (his father is from Glasgow), Cam had always imagined he'd live in the UK at some point. As it turned out, it was coffee that brought him here. He and his old surfing buddy James Gurnsey teamed up with Peter Hall, an ethical funds manager from Sydney. Peter had spent time in London on business and had always struggled to find a decent coffee. He knew there was a gap in the market. It was Peter who found the site on Berwick Street. He had an office in Soho and knew the area was a hotbed of creativity with interesting people from artists to musicians. Berwick Street is home to a lively street market, its stalls and barrows laden with fruit and vegetables and household goods lining the narrow street. He thought it would be perfect.

Cam and James arrived in London not quite knowing what to expect. "We wanted to create something we knew would take off," says Cam. And so they opened Flat White, a café focussing on well-made coffee using beans from Monmouth, one of London's established coffee roasters. They believed that the city was ready for this new style of coffee. How right they were.

Flat White quickly amassed a cool following of coffee worshipers. One such regular was James Hoffman. "We would talk about coffee," says Cam. "He knew his stuff—he really knew his stuff!" James went on to become the 2007 World Barista Champion, set up Square Mile Coffee Roasters in East London and now provides Flat White with their own blend of beans to use in the café.

The café takes its name from the espresso-based coffee that's a less frothy take on a cappuccino. "The flat white is a regional name for a certain type of coffee," Cam says. "It's about bringing

the milk down and dedicating it to espresso." It requires a certain skill from the barista. The milk must be steamed—or stretched—until it is completely smooth. "Essentially you're whipping the milk and messing with the lactose in it," Cam says.

He designed the counter backwards putting the espresso machine in the window by the door so it's the first thing that customers see. Cam and his team used latté art to demonstrate that they care about the whole process and as a means to get people talking about the coffee. "Then we'd direct them to the grinder, the beans . . . It was about education," Cam says.

The simple décor acts as a backdrop for the art on the walls that is usually for sale and changes

regularly. Flat White has been credited by Kiwis for recreating a slice of New Zealand in the heart of London. "We didn't go in with a plan. We just did what we knew," says Cam. Tables are tightly packed and at peak times it can be elbow-to-elbow. Customers tap away on iPads and mobiles (laptops seem somewhat clunky in the limited space) and music pumps from a speaker in the back corner.

Flat White isn't so much a place in which to while away an afternoon as a place to refuel with a top coffee. You won't find comfy sofas or cosy nooks to bed down into. Service is brisk—on occasion surly—but these guys are serious about the coffee they're making for you. Chances are you'll have to queue up at the counter but it'll be worth the wait. At Flat White the hidden extras are in the coffee itself.

A couple of years after opening Flat White, the demand for coffee was such that Cam opened a sister café, Milk Bar, a few roads away on Bateman Street. James returned to New Zealand to set up a boutique café and roastery near Christchurch, leaving Cam to run the show in London.

In June 2011 Cam added a Synesso Hydra to the line-up on the counter, a gleaming 4-group espresso machine from Seattle. The water can be preset to four different temperatures meaning four blends of coffee can be brewed at their optimum temperatures simultaneously. Cam also introduced a cold water drip coffee that slowly extracts the flavour of the beans without the acidity. It's served in a glass over ice. Cam is still very hands-on when it comes to making coffee. "I tend to be the guy who's pushing people off the machine. I'm an addict," he grins. "You're always learning with coffee. It's the best job in the world."

Browns of Brockley

5 Coulgate Street, Brockley SE4 2RW
020 8692 0722
Open: 7.30AM-6PM Mon-Fri, 9AM-5PM Sat, 10AM-4PM Sun
Rail: Brockley

Browns of Brockley, a little café opposite Brockley train station, is known for its great coffee. Owner Ross Brown and his small team can all make a mean coffee that's beautifully decorated with latté art. The coffee, chalked up on the wall, is by Square Mile Coffee Roasters and other guest roasters and you can buy coffee gadgets and bags of beans to take home. There is much grinding and hissing from the coffee machine and if you listen carefully you might hear the baristas discussing extraction times and mulling over flavour profiles and other technical

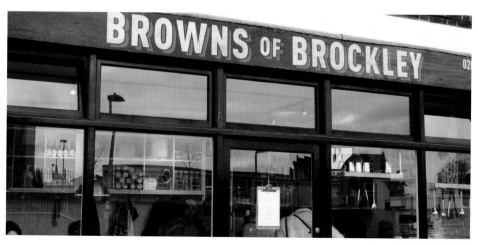

details. For Ross, artisan coffee is a combination of factors. "It's fresh coffee that's ethically sourced, focussing on brew recipes, steaming milk correctly, and having the equipment to meet those demands," he says.

Ross studied at the American Barista and Coffee School in Portland, USA, then worked for coffee roasters Darlington's in Vauxhall, South London. He learned everything he could about coffee, hanging out in Soho cafés while planning to open a coffee-bike business. He was living in New Cross, the next station along from Brockley, and used to walk down Coulgate Street where he noticed the For Sale sign in the window of what was then a deli. He abandoned his coffee-bike plans and took over the deli business. Soon after he gave the shop a re-fit and turned it into a café. The communal table that runs through the centre of the room is the old deli counter—the round hole cut into one end is where the cash register was wired in.

On weekends you're lucky to be able to find a seat in Browns, never mind two together, as locals stream in for their obligatory caffeine fix. Neighbors, friends, and strangers who meet at Browns and perhaps become friends, chat across the table and to the baristas. There is more seating along a small bar in the window and on a slouchy sofa at the back, though this is often occupied by Ludd, Ross's small dog. Hooks along one wall display ads for yoga classes, bass guitar lessons, and Spanish tuition, and local art for sale. If the café door is open and the wind's blowing in the right direction you can hear the train announcements on the platform across the road.

Unless you have something really pressing to attend to, it seems a shame to leave Browns after a single coffee. Even if further caffeine is not required, one of their colourful salads, sandwiches, croissants, or bagels filled with pastrami, mustard and gherkins or smoked salmon with cream cheese and capers—or a delightfully gooey brownie or cookie—deserve investigation. The food is freshly made by the Browns team in a kitchen on the other side of the railway tracks. It's walked over the footbridge during the course of the morning in a large flat box and unpacked into the window display and onto waiting customers' plates.

The backstreets of Brockley retain a villagey feel and laid-back vibe. Coulgate Street serves largely as a drop-off and pick-up point for the station and for cars cruising by in search of a parking space. It's probably one of the few remaining spots in London where a car might

triple-park and the driver dash in to order takeaway coffee. The staff from the cab office next-door to Browns pop their heads round the door at regular intervals and disappear back with their coffees, returning later with the empty cups. Next-door is another café, The Broca, with cupcakes in the window and hot drinks served in mismatched crockery. The emphasis on coffee is more evident at Browns yet each café's loyal following is proof that two similar outlets can co-exist quite happily.

Everyone who works at Browns is friendly and can-do. "I generally like to take on people who don't have coffee experience," says Ross. "Then you can just employ nice people." Nice people who become skilled baristas.

Climpson & Sons

67 Broadway Market, Hackney E8 4PH
020 7812 9829 www.webcoffeeshop.co.uk
Open: 8AM-5PM Mon to Fri,
8.30AM-5PM Sat, 9AM-4PM Sun
Rail: Cambridge Heath, London Fields,
Haggerston

IN 2004 the once thriving market stalls of Broadway Market, a narrow street in Hackney, wedged between London Fields and Regent's canal, returned to life. Now, every Saturday, you'll find around 80 stalls with offerings from food to fashion and a large serving of community spirit. Having survived the bombs of two World Wars, the buildings and character of this street are a true blend of old and new. In the shadow of the neighboring tower block, many of the street's previously run-down or derelict shops have reopened as cafés, delis, and other independent stores. Along from the ladders and mops piled up outside the ironmongers, you'll find a smart bookshop, an organic greengrocer's, a clothing boutique, and a handful of estate agents.

Needless to say, property prices have crept up accordingly. Today a local mum pushing a designer pram might walk alongside an old lady with her shopping trolley. Yet despite the young blood moving in, Broadway Market has retained both its sense of community and its edge.

Bethnal Green, the nearest Underground station, is a bit of a hike but there are Overground stations and free parking if you can find it on weekends on Broadway Market. Or, better still, jump on one of the many buses that run along Mare Street from Hackney Central station a few minutes away. Arrive at Broadway Market with an empty stomach and primed for your first caffeine hit of the day. You'll find fish and chips, kebabs, greasy spoon diners, and a pie 'n' mash shop (Fred Cooke's original shop opened in 1900 and continued to thrive throughout the century). There are also a couple of pubs including an old alehouse that is today a cracking boozer called the Cat & Mutton. It's been there since the late 1600s and originally was the Cattle & Shoulder of Mutton because of the farmers who used to call by with their animals on their way to market in the City.

And then there's coffee. Climpson & Sons was one of the first of the specialty cafés on Broadway Market, at the London Fields end, opposite the bakers. Large windows open onto the pavement and you can jostle for space at one of the tables on the pavement. Call in during the week and you'll be among a friendly crowd of freelancers and locals calling in on their way to work. Call in anytime and you'll be guaranteed a great cup of freshly roasted coffee, friendly service, and a selection of simple food that's made on site in the tiny corner kitchen behind the counter.

Before Ian Burgess set up Climpson & Sons he spent some time in Australia in the 1990s where he recalls hanging out at Sydney's beaches and drinking coffee. He worked in a café where a friend taught him the coffee basics, although at the time he admits to wondering what all the fuss was about. In 2000 he returned to the UK and decided to explore the coffee market. "I realized it was just chains," he says. He pounded the streets, targeting commercial spaces in airports and business parks, hoping to set up a coffee business on site. In the end he took a different tangent—he set up a market stall instead. With a thousand pounds to his name he bought a coffee machine and a grinder, found someone to roast coffee beans and established Burgil Coffee. He started making coffee at farmers' markets in West London and at food fairs and festivals and the business grew from there.

He started roasting his own beans in a unit in Camden Market that he shared with a sofa company. He taught himself. "It was trial and error," he remembers. Soon after, he started making coffee on a stall in Broadway Market on Saturdays. The street was dead during the week but the

Saturday farmers-style market was probably one of the busiest markets he had experienced. He did the stall for a year, by which time he knew he wanted to open a café with a roastery. In 2005 he gave up the unit in Camden and moved fully into the site on Broadway Market, inheriting the name Climpson & Sons from the previous occupier, a butcher's. Ian set about renovating the space, peeling everything back to the original features. Six weeks later, Climpson & Sons reopened as a café. Ian remembers the greatest challenge was getting the café established. "It was all word of mouth," he says. Following on from the success of Ian's market stall, Climpson & Sons took off.

At first they roasted in the back of a neighboring furniture shop (now a café-deli called La Bouche). Ian ran the café and roastery operation and over the next two years it grew and found its feet. By then he'd handed the stall over to another barista to run and moved the roastery into its current site in the gated mews a few doors down from the café. The roastery is crammed with foil packs, sacks of beans, and stashes of flat-packed boxes. They now roast for the café as well as wholesale—cafés, delis, restaurants, and events—and they still make coffee for festivals. The volume they roast is increasing every month. "We're literally popping out at the seams," Ian says. As well as roasting many single origin coffees, they roast for three blends including their seasonal blend that's served in the café. In the spring of last year your coffee would have hinted at caramel undertones with a gentle floral acidity. "It's a medium roast," explains head roaster Matt Ho. "If you roast too dark, you lose the nuances of the origin. Roast too light and it could be too acidic for espresso."

In terms of growing the operation, the best thing was to step away, Ian says, as it freed him up to concentrate on other aspects of the business. Today he has around 12 staff including a head barista, operations and accounts managers. Wholesale manager Danny Davies—who describes himself as "everything and nothing"—is responsible for increasing sales and keeping the coffee tasting good.

A while after opening Climpson & Sons, Ian recalls a time when the café was full of people and buzzing with life. "I sat outside with a coffee and went, wow, it's worked!"

Taylor Street Baristas

22 Brook Mews, Mayfair W1K 4DY
020 7629 3163 www.taylor-st.com
Open: 7.30AM-5PM Mon to Fri
Tube: Bond Street

IF A COFFEE'S NOT GOOD ENOUGH to serve at Taylor Street Baristas, the barista will make another. "We get so excited when we see a barista throw a coffee or milk away," says co-owner Laura Tolley. "We applaud it!" The same care and effort goes into the first coffee of the day as the last. Their beans, from Union Hand-Roasted, are re-blended every three months and they offer guest beans from other roasters. Taylor Street Baristas have a collection of espresso machines—including La Marzocco, Dalla Corte and Simonelli—across their eight cafés. At their café in Bank, located in a ground-floor unit of 26 storeys of financial and real estate businesses in the financial City of London, they're making over 1,000 coffees a day. Here they use a Synesso machine for their guest espresso as it's great for playing around with temperature and fun to work on, says Laura. The operation is sleek and smart—the menu's projected onto the wall above the large counter—and at lunchtime well-heeled office workers start to pour in. At the height of the lunchtime rush, you'll have to queue to order but service is friendly, you'll find a seat at one of the many communal tables, where you can tuck into quiche—sometimes still warm from the oven—sandwiches and salads.

Taylor Street Baristas was set up by Australian Tolley siblings Laura, Nick and Andrew. The café takes its name from a road in the Sydney suburb of Darlinghurst where they used to live. "It's a cool, vibrant spot. We loved it," says Laura. They moved over to the UK and came up with the idea of starting a concession in a store and in 2005 opened a café in Source, a gourmet food store in Richmond, West London.

The Tolleys have since expanded to over 50 staff spread across their seven other cafés—six in London and one in the seaside town of Brighton on the south coast. The Mayfair café, tucked down a quiet backstreet behind Bond Street station, opened in 2011. Laura took charge of the interior design, sourcing salvaged furniture and recycled fittings and fixtures. The look, she says, is rustic. The blackboard menu is framed in a wooden surround from a fireplace, the coat-stand was a find in a rural market, and the counter was fashioned from the garage doors of their grandmother's house in Ascot. "They are seriously old," Laura says. She found other furniture at an antiques market in Sunbury in West London. There are pretty plates and cake stands on the counter and art on the walls. One minute the café is ticking along quietly then, out of nowhere, noise levels start to rise and people queue at the counter. Coffee at Taylor Street Baristas is in demand all day long, it seems.

The Tolleys are an enviable mix of complimentary skills. Andrew, the coffee geek, lives in Brighton and comes up to London three days a week to oversee training and the technical side of things. Nick is the business-brains and Laura's the creative one, focussing on business branding and design. She's converted the garage next door to the Mayfair café into her office where she focusses on the website and menu design. The common thread that unites them—as well as their love of coffee—is their belief in the importance of being hands-on. "The customers like to see us," says Laura. "We keep our hand in the game. We keep in touch with our customers and see how the baristas are doing."

Each café has a small kitchen for baking muffins and other small bites but there is now a main kitchen operation that caters for all the cafés. Every morning at the crack of dawn, one of the kitchen staff pedals the food out on a pushbike with a trailer to the cafés at Shoreditch, Liverpool Street and Bank. "Come rain or shine," says Laura.

Recently they opened The Shed in East London's Shoreditch. It's a café in a kit shed that they bought off the internet, built in a day, and put in a car-park in probably the most obscure, hard-to-find location possible. They fitted it out with a counter and a couple of low tables and now serve a small, loyal customer base of local workers. 'It's an oasis in the middle of Shoreditch," says Laura.

As the business expanded, the Tolleys greatest challenge was to step back and hand over the running of each café to a manager. "You learn to de-stress, to let go a little," says Laura. Gone are the days when they used to wake in the night worrying about a coffee they'd sent out that day that wasn't quite perfect. "The cafés develop their own character and personality over time," she says. Now it feels like many of the staff are part of the family. Many customers are Australian and two regulars from the Richmond store were bridesmaids at Laura's wedding in 2011.

Sacred

13 Ganton Street, Soho W1F 9BL
020 7734 1415 **www.sacredcafe.co.uk**
Open: 7.30AM-8PM Mon to Fri,
10AM-7PM Sat and Sun
Tube: Oxford Circus, Piccadilly Circus

SACRED WAS FOUNDED BY New Zealanders Tubbs Wanigasekera and Matthew Clark who hit on the idea of bringing gourmet coffee to London. They opened their Ganton Street café in 2005, at almost exactly the same time that Flat White opened its doors a short walk away on Berwick Street. Suddenly London had two Kiwi-owned cafés that both focussed on high quality, artisan-style coffee. Matthew believes New Zealand has become recognized as a leader in the world's coffee-scene because of the country's geographical isolation. "No one's ever told us how a coffee should be," he says. The Antipodean flat white—espresso topped with steamed milk— is a good example of that. It's basically a bastardized cappuccino.

2005 was a significant turning point in London's coffee scene. Before the heavily branded chains introduced Londoners to a world of skinny lattés and syrupy flavourings, we'd all made do with instant coffee. Then coffee was on the rise of what became known as the Third Wave with a more artisan-style approach in terms of how it was sourced, presented, and tasted. Sacred's mission was simple: "A New Zealand style of coffee, with depth of flavour and latté art as standard," says Matthew. "We wanted a place with a really organic feel, where people could come and kill time. A haven from the high street. In New Zealand people go to cafés in the same way that people go to bars here. We wanted to create an environment that was accessible for anyone," he says.

Ganton Street, a small offshoot of Carnaby Street in Soho, seemed perfect for what they had in mind. The area is famous for its bars, restaurants, and fashion boutiques and was the place to be seen during the Swinging Sixties in London. Today Carnaby and its surrounding streets attract local workers, shoppers, and tourists in their thousands and if there's so much as a hint of sun, the tables outside the bars and cafés are teaming with customers soaking up the rays. Despite competition from around 20 or so other cafés in the immediate vicinity, Sacred is always busy. Yet when they first opened, Matthew remembers people putting their head round the door wondering what it was all about. They would ask whether they could just pop in for a coffee without having to buy food. Word soon spread that this was somewhere different and people returned in droves, bringing friends and partners. "Once the Brits get hold of something

new, they go nuts for it," Matthew smiles. Today in Sacred you're as likely to find a backpacker in flip-flops as an office-worker who's ducked away from his desk for a coffee. Weekends are manic with tourists and shoppers from nearby Oxford and Regent Streets spilling into this network of pedestrianized streets in search of smaller, independent stores.

Matthew and Tubbs have since opened five more cafés across London, including a small coffee kiosk in Kingly Court, moments from their Ganton Street café. They also now have a central kitchen in North London where all the baking's done. It's hearty food made with good ingredients. There are sandwiches, quiches, salads, and chewy Anzac biscuits. A piece of cake will arrive garnished with a berry coulis and cream. Then there's their famous lolly cake, a favourite at children's birthday parties in New Zealand. It's a mix of crushed malt biscuits, condensed milk, and chewy flourescent sweets, that's baked and rolled in coconut. "A lolly cake is dreadful!" Matthew smiles. "Approximately 150,000 calories a slice. It's possibly the sweetest thing ever. It has the capacity of breaking teeth." Yet it flies out of the door at all their cafés. "We have New Zealanders who burst into tears when they see it," he says. "We sell literally hundreds a week."

Sacred seems to attract staff who genuinely love their job. Asking customers how their day's going is second nature them. "Australasians have exceptional respect in the hospitality environment. Our staff have a real responsibility to the legend of that," Matthew says. He remembers learning how to make coffee, where over the course of five days, maybe four out of the thousand coffees he made was drinkable. "I am spectacularly crap at making coffee!" he laughs. Tubbs, on the other hand, is a dab hand behind the espresso machine and, as well as running Sacred, he owns a separate business that imports handmade espresso machines. Needless to say, you won't find Matthew behind the coffee machine—instead your coffee will be made by a trained barista with at least one year's experience.

Matthew and Tubbs first dipped their toes into the coffee market when they ran a coffee kiosk on the platform at Kensington Olympia underground station. "A windswept platform on a dead-end line, it was terrifying. We were broken into about every three days," says Matthew. Yet they used the experience as an opportunity to test their blend and refine the flavour of the coffee. Then they moved into Ganton Street and upped the scale of the operation.

Tubb's original occupation as an industrial designer accounted for his input in the café's layout and design, including the branding and logo. To fund the fit-out and the large financial guarantees required, Tubbs invested his personal savings from his career in motorsport and his espresso machine business. "I took a personal gamble," he says. Even still, there was no lavish budget and they did as much of the work that they could themselves. "We ran the wiring and built the furniture. It's the Kiwi can-do attitude," says Matthew. The Ganton Street café is furnished with artefacts that nod towards religious iconography. Chunky church candles flicker against the bare brick wall and the espresso machine sits proudly on top of an eighteenth century pulpit, a tongue-in-cheek reference to the café's name. "We wanted to create an oasis of calm. We're big on recycling and being creative," says Tubbs. It's the finer details—the stainless steel shakers for the iced coffees and the house tea blend which comes from Tubbs' great-great-grandfather's estate in Sri Lanka—that make Sacred unique.

The ground floor is perfect for people watching. Doors open fully and the café spills outside. Downstairs, by contrast, it's warm and cosy, a place to escape from the action on the street. "A lot of affairs are conducted down here. You see people spill apart when someone comes down the stairs," Matthew grins. The basement is a venue for community groups from book and sewing clubs to art exhibitions and fund-raising events.

A café needs time to bed in and evolve. It's not about chrome and having everything new and shiny. "Coffee is blackboards, personalities, and relationships," Matthew says. "And London's a coffee town now. It's a wonderful thing to be able to walk around and go, holy crap, there's so much here! You can't lie to customers anymore. They know if you're authentic. They can smell it."

Kaffeine

66 Great Titchfield Street, Fitzrovia W1W 7GJ
020 7580 6755 www.kaffeine.co.uk
Open: 7.30AM-6PM Mon to Fri,
9AM-6PM Sat, 9.30AM-5PM Sun
Tube: Oxford Circus, Great Portland Street,
Goodge Street, Tottenham Court Road

HEAD NORTHWARDS UP Great Titch-field Street, leaving behind the shopping frenzy and mayhem of Oxford Street, and within moments you'll start to shake off the crowds. Shop windows become smaller, fashion brands less assuming, and businesses are inter-spersed with sandwich bars, pubs and other small eateries. Just as you might consider turning back, chances are you'll have just about reached Kaffeine.

Kaffeine sits comfortably among a handful of long-established, old-school cafés doing simi-lar sandwich-style food, yet without the coffee element or service that Kaffeine's Australian founder Peter Dore-Smith had in mind when he was planning his venture. "What we wanted to do was focus on the food and coffee and allow customers to escape from their world for five minutes or half an hour, then leave and say, right, I feel better now," he says. Today Kaffeine is one of the busiest cafés in London, producing in excess of 500 coffees a day. It's fair to say that a great number of people have felt better for walking through the café's door.

Peter has certainly hit on a winning formula that's definitely more by design than by chance. At 3 o'clock on an average weekday afternoon in Kaffeine, you will barely notice the music

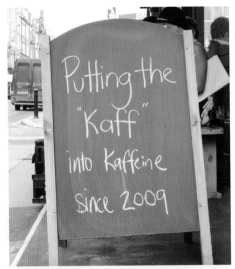

beneath the lively conversation and frenetic whirring of the coffee grinders. Staff, quick on their feet, flit between tables, ferrying out coffees, pouring water, and clearing tables as the next customer jumps in to claim a perch. Customers queue from door to counter and yet still people keep coming. Peter is very much part of the action, his focus unwavering as he takes orders and darts off to clear empty cups.

The drinks menu is displayed on a board above the counter and lists coffees from flat whites to piccolos. There are also Sweet Things—hot chocolate, mocha, and iced coffee—and a fresh mint tea called Moroccan whisky. Yet despite all these offerings, nine out of ten customers go for coffee.

Peter grew up in Melbourne and coffee went on to play a significant part in his career. He spent three years in London in the mid-1990s and on returning to Melbourne, he noticed a definite shift in the café scene. "Coffee was becoming more important. Cafés were more modern," he says. He did a teacher-training course in Food and Beverage Services where coffee was one of the main elements.

In 2005 he returned to London, this time

with his wife Rita, where they soon realized there were few places to find a decent coffee. In other words, there was the potential to set up something new. They spent much of their spare time travelling round, checking out other cafés. "I used my hospitality experience to see how places worked or didn't work," Peter says. At the time, he was working at Lord's Cricket Ground, responsible for around 600 catering staff at all the major events. The dream of opening his own place was never far from his thoughts. "The whole time I was planning and saving and talking through my ideas with people," he says.

He started looking into locations. "We looked at the demographic of people who would be attracted to good coffee and the type of food we were planning to do. We looked at various

locations and industries," he says. Fitzrovia, just north of Oxford Street, seemed the best fit, bubbling with creatives working in animation, film, fashion, music, and advertising. The BBC's Broadcasting House is a couple of minutes' walk away. There's a sprinkling of residents, too, in the flats above the row of shops, bars, and cafés on Great Titchfield Street. It was Rita who came across the location and came up with the name for the café. Hayden Smart, an old friend of Peter and Rita, invested in the business as a silent partner. Some other friends devised the logo and Peter loved the way the letters flowed. On 14 August 2009, Kaffeine opened for business.

They chose Square Mile coffee as Peter had been going along to cupping (tasting) sessions at the East London roastery. "I really wanted to go with those guys, so I asked James Hoffman if he could supply us," Peter says. Kaffeine serves the current seasonal blend and a decaf, ground to order. They have two grinders—an Anfim for the decaf and a higher-speed Robur for the popular espresso blend. "The Robur has an inbuilt fan to keep the motor cool so it can grind in three seconds without overheating. We're now saving four seconds per coffee, which when you consider we're doing over 400 a day . . . " he says. It's a saving nearly half an hour, just on grinding alone. The Synesso Cyncra espresso machine, referred to on Kaffeine's website as "the holy grail of espresso machines," is one of only a handful in operation in the UK. "We don't know how long it will last—like a car, it depends on how it's treated. Luckily the girls are really proud of it, so they look after it," Peter says.

Catherine Seay was lead barista at Kaffeine from the day it opened until 2011. "We're lucky to be able to work with all this equipment," she said of her time there. "Our goal is to give out consistently good coffee. You need to care about each one." For the baristas, it comes down to tasting, tasting, tasting. When it comes to training other baristas, the most important quality is to have the right attitude, Catherine believes. She learned her craft working in coffee shops back home in Queensland. "In Australia you can get a reasonable coffee in most places, whereas in the UK you've got either a lot of bad coffee or super-specialized places. There's nothing in between," she says.

Coffee at Kaffeine is made with a double shot unless otherwise requested and flat whites are the most popular choice. With each new blend, Square Mile gives Kaffeine ballpark figures to work with— the temperature and the weight—then it's for them to fine tune it. The baristas keep a daily coffee log, a rule-lined exercise book that's stained with coffee, to record extractions times, roasting details, weights and volumes, and most crucially, tasting notes of how the coffee is every single day. "Sweet, juicy orangey taste, complex but vibrant," reads one entry. "Candied fruit, almond taste, less berry than spring, better with milk," was the first day of the 2010 summer blend.

As for the décor, Peter deliberately set out to create different spaces within the room. The area at the back consists of small wooden blocks that double-up as seats or tables. The rest of the seating is at high tables—former school laboratory tables—looking out onto the street or facing the counter where you can watch the baristas at work. Walls are white-washed and exposed brick.

Pendant lights are suspended along the counter and bare bulbs dangle down at the window. It's certainly a place to linger over a second coffee, though cyber addicts will find there's no Wi-Fi. "I didn't want people sitting here all day or for it to turn into an internet café for students," Peter says. Kaffeine is more about conversation; an excuse to pick up a newspaper; and, above all, the appreciation of a great cup of coffee and a plate of food that's been made with love and care. The menu includes colourful salads, quiches, and sandwiches, freshly made in the kitchen downstairs. It sells out fast—soon after lunch it's mostly gone.

Most people who work at Kaffeine tend to be Australians or New Zealanders. "I'm very particular about who I take on. They must have experience making coffee," says Peter. In its first year of operation, Kaffeine was awarded Runner-up for Best Cup of Coffee in London by London's weekly Time Out magazine. "Reviews help to build a reputation and get you your internet hits. If you do well in Time Out business can go through the roof," says Peter. "But it's the customers who come here—some of them three times a day—who are most important to us."

· 2 ·

TEA

WHETHER IT'S WHITE WITH THREE SUGARS or a delicate floral infusion, the simple pleasure derived from a cup of tea is as relevant today as it was in the middle of the seventeenth century, when the beverage was introduced to Britain.

Tea might seem quintessentially British, but the custom of drinking tea was invented in China over 5,000 years ago by Emperor Shen Nung. The legend goes that when leaves from a burning tea twig accidentally landed in the cauldron of boiling water that his servant was preparing, the emperor decided to taste the infusion and the famous beverage was born.

Tea was first shipped over to Europe by Dutch merchants in the early seventeenth century. It soon became a popular beverage among the nobility and aristocratic classes in Western Europe, including Portugal. It was tea-lover Catherine of Braganza, the Portuguese wife of King Charles II, who is credited with making tea fashionable among the British nobility and across Britain's wealthy classes.

The first reference that tea was permeating into Britain's public domain was in a 1658 newspaper advert proclaiming that it was available at a coffeehouse in Sweeting's Rents in the City of London, on what is now the site of the Royal Exchange building in Cornhill. Fast-forward over 300 years and tea is Britain's favourite drink. The UK's Tea Council estimates that by 9 o'clock on any given morning the nation will have drunk its way through around 60 million cups of tea, 96 percent of which will have been brewed in bags.

Every tea-drinker has his or her preferred method of making tea: a quick dunk with a bag or a more leisurely infusion of loose leaves; in a cup or mug; and with or without milk. Tea purists

might use filtered water to eliminate cloudiness and meticulously time the infusion according to the type of tea and the size of the leaves.

You'll be hard pressed to find a café in London that doesn't serve tea. For some, though, it's at the heart of their business. Depending on the café or tearoom, you can accompany your cuppa with anything from a simple slice of cake to afternoon tea, that decadent, tiered affair of finger sandwiches and little cakes. Yet however you choose to take your tea, one thing's certain—you'll be among thousands of others across the country who are also indulging at that very moment.

Orange Pekoe

3 White Hart Lane, Barnes SW13 0PX
020 8876 6070 www.orangepekoeteas.com
Open: 7.30AM-5.30PM Mon to Fri,
9AM-5.30PM Sat to Sun
Rail: Barnes Bridge

ASK SELF-CONFESSED TEA BUFF Marianna Hadjigerogiou, owner of Orange Pekoe, which tea is the best in the world and she'll say there's no such thing. Rather it's a matter of personal taste. "People say that Darjeeling is the Champagne of tea but I disagree. My favourite's a Ceylon from Kenilworth Estate. It's lovely in the afternoon and I drink it with a little honey," she says.

Orange pekoe is a high grade, large leaf tea from which the Barnes tearoom takes its name. Marianna's love of tea stems from her childhood. "At home there was always a big pot of tea on the go with lots of yummy food. I often really craved that place," she says.

A few years ago she became fed up with the meagre selection of teas on offer at cafés for tea drinkers. "As a nation of tea drinkers it was actually quite appalling what we had to offer. There were the café chains and five star hotels and nothing in between. Coffee was so in and being executed so well." So she decided to do something about it. She and her husband Achilleas—both from catering backgrounds—decided to open their own tearoom. First though, Marianna spent a year researching and studying tea. She travelled around Europe—where the main tea-importers are based—and became friends with tea expert, writer, and historian Jane

Pettigrew (her "fairy godmother"), who introduced her to a whole host of other tea gurus. She hung out with old-school tea merchants. "They were all so enthusiastic and supportive that someone was breathing new life into it," Marianna says.

Then Marianna and Achilleas found the site in Barnes, West London's Thames-side suburb with its village green and handsome boutiques and delis. "I didn't want to open on a busy high street. When Barnes came up in conversation, I knew it was the right place to be," she says. "We drove past the shop when it was already under offer but even then I knew it was the one." As luck had it, the deal fell through, so the site went to the couple after all. She roped in her mum and brother to help and opened their doors in April 2006. "Stupidly on a Saturday!" she laughs. "We were packed within five minutes and spent the next three years chasing our tails."

The lovely room at the front of the tearoom is lined with tea caddies. You're encouraged to open them and smell the leaves within. Walk through to a narrow conservatory-like room with a glass ceiling and rows of little tables along the walls. It's the kind of place where locals pop in throughout the day and others come from further afield on weekends. Most of the time the tearoom is full of women and mums. Settle down at a table and order a pot of tea and a bite to eat (breakfasts include hot crumpets or eggs Florentine and lunches are soups, tarts, and salads) and you'll soon start to unwind.

Orange Pekoe is famed for its afternoon teas—for which you will need to book—and there is absolutely nothing stuffy about them. It's afternoon tea without the dress code. "If people want to have afternoon tea in a pair of jeans, they can," says Marianna. Whatever you choose to wear, tea at Orange Pekoe is a civilized affair. You'll be shown to a table where a tea specialist—a sommelier, no less—will help you choose the right tea to suit your mood from the 90 or so listed in a little book. An assortment of freshly-cut sandwiches and little cakes will arrive on a tiered stand. And if you feel like pushing the boat out, indulge in a glass of Champagne, too.

Teas are divided into the five main processing methods—black, oolong, green, yellow, and white—and there are herbal and fruit infusions, from whole organic rosebuds and chrysanthemum flowers to a zesty, refreshing Wake Up blend of lemongrass, apple pieces, orange peel, and blackberry leaves. Each tea is prepared according to the recommended brewing temperature and timing to bring out the best flavours. "Each tea has its own lesson," Marianna says. Teas are infused and strained at the bar, so they're ready to drink when they arrive at the table and won't continue brewing in the pot. "There are some exceptions but generally you would never leave tea leaves in the pot," Marianna says. All teas on the menu cost the same as she hopes to encourage her customers to be adventurous in their choices.

According to Marianna, a teacup has to be thin bone china and her green teas and herbal infusions are served in Moroccan style glasses. Crockery is key to the enjoyment of tea. After all, there's little point serving a fine tea in a clunky cup. All the crockery in Orange Pekoe is for sale. "Everything used to be vintage and antique but we soon learnt from that mistake," Marianna says, recalling all the breakages. "We now have everything made for us down south."

And coffee lovers won't leave disappointed, either. Orange Pekoe certainly isn't just about tea. The level of coffee is just as high, says Marianna, and credits coffee as being key to the tearoom's success. Coffee is Achilleas's domain and their baristas Alfie and Christina have been there from day one. "We invest in our staff and are artisans in what we do," says Marianna.

Royal Teas

76 Royal Hill, Greenwich, SE10 8RT
020 8691 7240 www.royalteascafe.co.uk
Open: 9.30AM-5.30PM Mon to Fri,
10AM-6PM Sat, 10AM-5.30PM Sun
Rail/DLR: Greenwich, Cutty Sark

MEANDER UP ROYAL HILL, leaving behind the beating heart of Greenwich and its vibrant market, day-trippers, and tourists, and you'll pass an impossibly quaint row of shops. There's a traditional butcher; a cheese shop with breads and pastries in the window; The Creaky Shed with its baskets of fruit and vegetables lined up outside; and La Fleur, a florist and teashop (see page 76). Tucked around the corner in a side street is The Fishmonger, a modern wet fish counter with plump lemons and bunches of parsley on standby. If you were lucky enough to live near Royal Hill you'd never need to set foot in a supermarket again.

A little further on up the hill, past a couple of pubs, you'll find Royal Teas. It's a tiny tearoom with just a couple of tables outside and a few more within. On the wall inside are old-style coffee dispensers (beans are from local Lewisham roasters Herbert & Ward) and rows of metal tins containing loose-leaf teas. There's an old set of scales for weighing out leaves and beans, and staff will scoop them into little brown bags for you to take home.

The tearoom itself is essentially a front and back room knocked into one. Walls are painted

orange and purple with bare-brick emerging through receding swirls of plaster. The window at the back offers a glimpse into the leafy garden behind. Step down into the low-ceilinged room and you might find Royal Teas owner Ray Voce behind the counter or in the little kitchen at the back. Before he set up his own business, Ray used to work as an airline steward. "Oh, I've had hundreds of jobs," he laughs. "I was also a mathematics teacher in a secondary school. That was all very stressful so I quit teaching and worked as a waiter in a restaurant. I quite liked that, so I started looking for a café to run." One of the directors at the restaurant owned the freehold to the building where Royal Teas was already operating. The lease was available and she urged him to take it.

So Ray took over the business. That was back in 1999. "It was very cliquey at the time, very intimidating. All the customers had their own prices. And you couldn't see for the cigarette smoke." Ray moved the builders in and set about putting his own stamp on the place. So much for his shoestring budget—the builders knocked through the chimneybreast and the ceiling fell in! "I'd only been here two weeks and thought, what on earth am I doing? We had to rehouse the upstairs tenants for six months and completely redo their flat. People would walk past the menu outside and change it to Rubble & Squeak and Lintel Soup!"

He decided to stick with the café's original name as it was already established in the area. "The old customers used to like sitting at the bar but there was none of that anymore," he smiles. "And we banned smoking before the no-smoking law came in." Yet the old customers still came. He decided to keep the menu largely vegetarian ("I was less likely to poison anyone") and designed the menu himself by researching ideas from other cafés and choosing the bits he liked. Breakfasts include waffles with maple syrup, porridge, and cooked breakfasts on weekends. There are juices and milkshakes. Lunches are simple—soups, savoury crêpes, and filled baguettes. Portions are generous and prices are astonishingly reasonable. "I keep prices low even though I won't buy cheap ingredients," Ray says. "I want people to get more than they'd expect." Teas are served by the pot for one, two or more, on small silver trays with retro cups and saucers. Cakes are sold by the slice with cream or ice cream or whole to take home.

After a few years of trading, Ray was forced to tweak the menu to comply with the no-cook licence enforced by the council which stated he was only allowed to reheat food and not to cook from scratch. Then Ray came up with a better solution—he and an old friend opened another café, The Brockley Mess, a couple of miles away between Brockley and Crofton Park. So now the team at the Mess do all the cooking and baking—from hollandaise to carrot cake—and bring it over to Royal Teas where it's finished off.

At lunchtime every table hums with conversation. There's no need to queue up at the counter to order—it's table service and staff flit from table to table, order pad in hand. The customers are a varied mix. "We get a few writers in here, novelists, local residents, and workers. Plus quite a lot of tourists and dancers from the Greenwich studios down the road. Some people come in twice a day so I get to hear all the gossip," Ray grins. "And there are two customers who are so regular that if they don't come we have to ring them or go and knock on their doors to make sure they're okay!"

The Tea Rooms

153-155 Stoke Newington Church Street,
Stoke Newington N16 0UH
020 7923 1870 www.thetearooms.org
Open: 11AM-6PM Mon to Fri,
11AM to 6.30PM Sat and Sun
Rail: Stoke Newington

I F YOU VISIT Isabelle Allfrey's tearoom on a weekend you can enjoy one of her gorgeous afternoon teas, a selection of sandwiches, cakes, and homemade scones with homemade jam (which she also sells by the jar). "We started doing afternoon tea on Mother's Day one year and now it's just so popular. We also do birthdays, bachelorette parties, baby showers . . . I did underestimate how many mums there were in Stoke Newington!" Isabelle laughs.

Cakes are Isabelle's passion. Many of those on the counter are old family recipes, passed down to Isabelle from her mother and grandmother. On any given day you're likely to find her great aunts Vera and Doris's gingerbread, traditional Victoria sandwich, chocolate layer cake, lemoncake, and carrot cakes. And chances are you'll find Isabelle in the kitchen, sleeves rolled up, whisking up a cake mix. "I like being in the kitchen," she smiles. She's a great believer in quality, traditional ingredients, so when it comes to her cakes you know she won't have skimped on the butter, sugar, and eggs. You can order celebration cakes for weddings, christenings and birthdays from The Tea

Rooms that are always beautifully decorated, some hand-painted in elaborate designs. "I can't take the credit for them!" says Isabelle. "Another lady called Leigh does the more intricate cake decorating for me." In addition to the cakes, savoury options include soups, sandwiches, salads, and tarts that are all handmade on site.

And then there are the many teas, chalked-up on the wall by the counter. Take your pick from black, green, white, chamomile flowers, basket of berries, or peppermint. It's all loose-leaf and served in pots and is available for takeout in bags and boxes, to brew at home or to give away as gifts.

Isabelle's a true Stoke Newington local. She grew up down the road from The Tea Rooms then trained as a chef at Westminster College. She went on to work as a pastry chef in private clubs and in private and royal households. She once even baked for the Queen at Kensington Palace—an elaborate centrepiece covered in over-the-top sparklers that was wheeled out on a trolley. She remembers the atmosphere as buzzing and the kitchen was told only at the last minute who their guest of honor was going to be.

She then hung up her apron for a while and took a desk job in catering recruitment. "I was craving to get back to the kitchen," she remembers. She'd always toyed with the idea of opening a café. Her mum, Anne Wilkinson, had started collecting pottery and glassware, hunting down pieces at markets, auctions, and fleamarkets. They decided to combine their skills and open a tearoom celebrated for its cakes and pastries that sold vintage pottery. They found a site—a former Thai restaurant—on Stoke Newington Church Street and converted it into the tearoom, installing a baking oven and a huge mixer in the new kitchen. They opened in August 2007 with Isabelle and Anne working all kinds of crazy hours to get it off the ground.

Clissold Park, just up the road from The Tea Rooms, is a favourite of local dog walkers, joggers and nature lovers. "I love the villagey feel of the area," Isabelle says. "Then you hit the high street and it's a great Turkish community, moving into Afro Caribbean towards Dalston. Here in Church Street you get a bit of both." Customers are mainly locals and many are regulars. During the week you'll get the mum-and-baby crowd plus freelancers, such as photographers and writers, who settle down with their laptops. Weekends bring more families and young professionals who live nearby but maybe work in town during the week. The tearoom is also used as a venue for local

groups and if you fancy trying your hand at decorating cupcakes, you can sign up for one of The Tea Rooms' cake decorating classes.

In 2010 the shoe shop next door came up for lease and Isabelle and Anne decided to take it on. They knocked through to create a larger space, then opened up the walled courtyard garden at the back. The interior is simple and uncluttered with pottery displays on shelves, tea-sets and cake stands in the windows. And for the many parents who visit, there are the all essential high-chairs, baby-changing area, and lots of space for strollers.

For regulars—and anyone else—who can't get enough of Isabelle's baking, she and her mum decided to share some of their family recipes in a book called Secrets of The Tea Rooms which you can buy at the café. But if you ever find yourself in Stoke Newington, call in to see Isabelle for a taste of the real thing.

Yumchaa

35 Parkway, Camden NW1 7PN
020 7209 9641 www.yumchaa.co.uk
Open: 8AM-8PM Mon to Fri,
9AM-8PM Sat and Sun
Tube: Camden Town, Mornington Crescent

"IT SOUNDS REALLY CORNY," says Huong Hoang co-owner of teashop Yumchaa, "but tea is for every occasion. For celebrating and commiserating. I start the day with an English breakfast tea. How I end it depends on how the day's gone . . . "

The Yumchaa on Parkway in Camden (there are also Yumchaa teashops on Berwick Street, Soho, and in Camden Lock) is a large, light space with huge windows that look out onto the pavement. For over 50 years the site was home to an exotic pet store called Palmers and the listed shop sign, advertising monkeys and talking parrots, remains. Palmers relocated across the road and Huong, her sister Trinh, and Trinh's husband Sean transformed the space into Yumchaa.

Inside you'll find an assortment of tables, chairs, and comfy sofas. Many of the tea-drinking customers—local residents, old and young, from Goths to vicars, families and tourists—are plugged into laptops while others come to sit around, chat or read. A large skylight floods the back area. "We love bright spaces," says Huong. "It's just somewhere that you can come and enjoy a fantastic cup of tea."

All the tea in Yumchaa is loose-leaf, made with filtered water and poured through strainers into china cups. "Bags might be good for convenience because they brew quickly but the leaves are too small to hold much flavour. It's just tea dust," says Huong. A loose-leaf tea promises far more flavour. "It's known as the agony of the leaf—the way the leaf unfurls as it steeps. It's like me waking up in the morning. I'm a tea-leaf!" she laughs. Their blends are in demand across the globe—they've even posted teas to South Korea.

One of the Yumchaa team will make you a tea that is green, white, black, or red (the red is fruit and flowers, so technically isn't a tea at all, only it's drunk in the style of tea). And to

help you decide which tea is right for you, stick your nose into the forty or so little jugs on the counter that contain a sample of each blend—Soho Spice, Midnight Grey, Regent's Park, Lemon Sherbet—before you order a pot. And to go with the teas there's a selection of sandwiches for toasting, and lovely homemade cakes, all freshly made.

Trinh and Sean met while studying at London School of Economics. After graduating, they borrowed some money, bought some tea, and set up a market stall on Portobello Road, West London. The stall was a hit, so they opened a couple more and in 2006 opened their first tea-shop in Camden Lock, London's famous open-air market. Soon after, they opened a second

shop in Berwick Street, Soho, then a third on Parkway. They love the relaxed feel of Camden, the strong sense of community and the visitors who flock to the area on weekends. They all live and breathe tea. Trinh and Sean even had a working honeymoon visiting tea gardens and estates in China, Nepal, and India.

They don't have the space to blend their own teas so they devise flavour combinations and have their tea blenders make them up. All the ingredients are real. "It's not just strawberry flavour—it's the actual strawberry, the fruit, the leaves," Huong says. She spends most of her time on the day-to-day operations and dreaming up new blends. "And we've been writing the website for years. But then we get sidetracked and come up with new teas. The fun stuff," she smiles.

· 3 ·

MORE THAN A CAFÉ

THERE IS SOMETHING RATHER LOVELY about finding a café tucked within another shop. Being invited to sit down and relax with a cup of tea and a plate of food among wares such as antiques, fresh flowers or books means you're likely to stay a little longer and leave feeling rejuvenated.

It can make the perfect place for a rendez-vous as there's twice as much under one roof. After you've caught up over food and drink, you can get down to the serious business of browsing— or vice versa. And for the owners, it's a win-win, too. By combining passions that feed into each other, they attract clientele they may not otherwise have reached.

Whether your primary motive for going is for sustenance or shopping, a café that shares a space with another enterprise can be a marvellous marriage. Here are some of London's best pairings.

Notes Music & Coffee

31 St Martin's Lane, WC2N 4ER
020 7240 0424 www.notesmusiccoffee.com
Open: Mon-Wed 7.30AM-9PM, Thurs-Fri
7.30AM-10PM, Sat 9AM-10PM, Sun 10AM-6PM
Tube/rail: Charing Cross,
Leicester Square, Covent Garden

NOTES ON St Martin's Lane is a gourmet café and music and movies store that specializes in classical, world, and jazz music and ballet and opera. Its central location by Trafalgar Square makes it the perfect stop for coffee-loving commuters who arrive into Charing Cross station from the South East. For shoppers, theatre-goers and day-trippers, weary from pounding the streets of Covent Garden, Soho, and beyond, it offers a welcome respite from the West End crowds. In the Autumn of 2011, a second branch of Notes opened in Wellington Street, a few minutes' walk away on the other side of Covent Garden. Both stores offer excellent coffee, fine wine, and food, so pull up a chair, have your spirits lifted by soothing music, a well-made coffee, and a slice of cake, then browse among the rows of CDs and DVDs that line the shelves.

Notes does coffee particularly well. Co-owners Robert Robinson and Fabio Ferreira have well and truly stamped their expertise behind the bar where baristas analyze extractions and run through tasting notes with customers. Rob used to run a coffee van in Paris. In 2008, he franchised the business, moved to London, and set up the van in Strutton Ground, a lively street

market near St James's. Coffee-mad Fabio, a barista from Brazil, became a customer and the pair decided to combine their love of coffee and go into partnership. Rob left the franchise and together they launched Flat Cap Coffee Co, a coffee cart that continues to operate in the same market.

At Notes there is excellent espresso to be had from the stunning La Marzocco Strada, but the focus here is on filter coffee. Pull up a stool at the brew bar—an extension of the main counter—and watch the barista pour hot water in a steady, circular motion into freshly ground beans that have been weighed to the nearest gram. It's like being back in the science lab at school, only here the potions are a lot more delicious. "Filter coffee is the new star," says Rob. "Behind all the intricacies of the brew bar is the simple aim to produce the tastiest possible coffees for our customers. It's amazing how many flavours can be found in filter coffee. Our brew bar is about building an appreciation for this under-appreciated side of coffee."

Each coffee is matched to a "precision brewing" method from filters to siphons to best bring out its flavours. Hot water is poured from a super-insulated aluminium kettle and every extraction

is timed to the nearest second. "It's great as people can see how easy it is," says Rob. In truth, the kit may be easy to install at home but it's down to the skill of the baristas who make it appear effortless. The result? A cup of coffee with flavours so complex, it's comparable to a fine wine.

The idea for the brew bar came from Penny University, a pop-up bar devised by former World Barista Champion James Hoffman and owner of Square Mile Coffee Roasters. James timed Penny University's opening with the World Barista Championships that were hosted for the first time in London in 2010, a crazy caffeine-fuelled week in June when the world's top baristas and coffee professionals hunted down the capital's best brews.

The weekly-changing coffee menu consists of traceable single origin beans and blends from specialist roasters along with the seasonal blend from Square Mile. With all these fabulous beans flying around, it's no wonder the baristas at Notes have four grinders on the go. Tea lovers needn't miss out either—there's a small menu of loose leaves that's perfect if you fancy a less caffeinated brew in the afternoon or evening. And should you deviate from the brew bar towards the food, you'll find seasonal salads and sandwiches with flavour combinations that are so inventive, you'll be instantly hooked—and possibly have to order another coffee to go with it.

Alan and Marion Goulden head up the music and movies side of Notes. During the 1980s, 1990s, and 2000s they ran leading specialist music stores MDC. The chain has since closed its doors but the Gouldens retained their shop on St Martin's Lane that had specialised in opera and ballet because of its location next to the English National Opera (ENO). They extended the space by removing a plasterboard wall and, to their delight, revealed a spectacular skylight and large mirrors set into the wall at the back. The Gouldens had always fancied combining their love of opera with coffee and this additional space gave them the idea to incorporate a café into the shop. A mutual friend introduced them to Robert and Fabio and, after a complete re-fit, 31 St Martin's Lane opened its doors in November 2010 as Notes.

A row of small tables opposite the counter leads to communal tables the back of the room and an enormous spider-like spotlight structure suspended beneath the skylight. Shelves are lined with CDs and DVDs while classic films, ballets, or operas are played out on flat screens. The Notes Underground sign above a door leads to a basement that's an Aladdin's cave of musical treasures.

In February 2011, Rob's original coffee van from Paris was resurrected and set up for business again, this time in a churchyard just off Fleet Street in the City. It was rechristened Coffee By The Clock (now a cart called Flat Cap Fleet Street) because of its position under a seventeenth century clock. In Autumn 2011 Rob and Fabio launched another coffee-cart in Borough Market at London Bridge. They're all great for coffee but if you're after a relaxing experience, too, then head to Notes.

La Fleur

18 Royal Hill, Greenwich SE10 8RT
020 8305 1772 www.la-fleur.co.uk
Open: 7AM-4.30PM Mon-Sat, 11AM-3PM Sun
Rail/DLR: Greenwich, Cutty Sark

To GO TO La Fleur for a pot of tea or a bite to eat is to idle away a peaceful moment. Set in a row of shops that include a traditional butcher's, a greengrocer's, and a cheese shop, this stretch of Royal Hill is off the beaten track from the heart of Greenwich and somehow seems a little lost in time. Inside La Fleur, you might imagine that you're in a sleepy village in France as you sit among others who talk quietly at old wooden tables arranged over creaky floorboards. You may even be tickled over your shoulder by the foliage hanging from baskets on the ceiling and around the windows. But this all adds to the charm of this beautiful little florist and teashop.

La Fleur is a family business run by Monique Ferrari and her daughter Rebecca. Monique lives upstairs, Rebecca and her son live nearby and Monique's other children Fabien and Gwen live locally, too. The Ferrari family came to England from Johannesburg, South Africa, in the mid-1990s and ran a deli in Rotherhithe, along the river to the West of Greenwich. In 2000 they took over an old florist on Royal Hill, an empty shell of a building. The family set about changing the style of the flowers from that of the previous business and transformed the space at the back into a tea garden. Monique, who is French, used to work as a florist in Paris. She and her family drew also on their catering experience from running a restaurant in South Africa.

Go through the old door that leads to a secret garden at the back of La Fleur and you may even spy Mimi, the resident cat. Crunching your way across the stones, admire an assortment of potted plants in the most original of places, including a bathtub, atop an old sewing machine and dotted along the grill of a barbecue. Don't be tempted to take one up to the counter, though,

as the plants in the tea garden are Monique's and aren't for sale. Sit among them, instead, and breathe in the scents of this tranquil garden.

Customers at La Fleur are a mixed bunch of locals from Greenwich mums and choreographers from the nearby Greenwich Dance Agency to barristers and doctors. Some customers even head over from the Isle of Dogs across the river. "People seem to stumble upon us," says Rebecca. "We call them our La Fleur Club, our regulars who come in everyday for coffees and lunches." They also have a smattering of tourists, thanks to their inclusion in guidebooks, from Danish to Japanese. No single day is typical. "It's so unpredictable," says Rebecca. "Weekends are generally busier—but you never know."

The menu is simple but the food is not to be rushed. To hurry here would be to miss the point. Monique sets the plates down at tables with a *bon appetit*. There are sandwiches and toasted paninis with saucisson, paté or brie. Monique makes a French onion soup and quiches, tarts, and gateaux are made by a local lady called Odette, a mother of four who spent several years in France. Vegetables and greens come from the delightfully named The Creaky Shed, the greengrocer's next door. "We found a menu that works for us. It's a balance of doing the flowers," says Rebecca. "We wanted to keep it small. We don't have a lot of space and it's not a big kitchen."

As for the florist-side of the business, customers tend to go to La Fleur for the rustic potted plants. Fresh flowers are available on Thursdays through the weekend and there are more during the winter when people aren't growing much in their gardens. "Our flowers are whimsical," says Rebecca, "Wild, traditional peonies, spray roses . . . "

Apart from their website, they've never had to do any advertizing. "I think the charm of this place is the French feel," says Rebecca. "People say they feel really relaxed when they leave. It's calming."

The Deptford Project Café

121-123 Deptford High Street, Deptford SE8 4NS
07545 593279 www.thedeptfordproject.com
Open 10AM-5.30PM Mon, Tues and Thurs, 9AM-5.30PM Weds, Fri and Sat, 10AM-4.30PM Sun
Rail/DLR: Deptford, Deptford Bridge

IN AN OLD RAILWAY YARD in the heart of Deptford in South East London you'll find a 1960s South Eastern Trains carriage that's home to The Deptford Project Café. Set up in 2008 by Rebecca Molina in partnership with independent property developers Cathedral Group, The Deptford Project is more than a café—it's about the regeneration of Deptford. A creative hub where people can go to eat, talk, and relax, it serves as a community space where locals and visitors can have their say about how the area evolves.

The carriage doors open out onto a decked area where you can sit among the plants and plastic pink flamingos and feast on homemade salads and bruschettas and drink coffee in the sun. The carriage and the surrounding space also acts as a venue for events and activities, including outdoor supper parties, exhibitions, cinema nights, theatre productions, and pop-up markets. The old railway arches behind the carriage have become studios and workshops for local craftspeople and the listed carriage ramp, first used in 1836 to enable trains to reach the station, is being restored.

Creating The Deptford Project has been a rewarding journey for Rebecca. At the time of its conception, she was running a multimedia design agency in the area. When the land around the old railway arches was sold, she approached Cathedral Group and proposed turning it into a temporary café and a creative space. Instead of shutting people out with hoarding, The Deptford Project would invite the community in and involve them with the area's regeneration. It would breathe life into a space that had stood derelict and unloved. "Developers have a reputation of coming in and knocking things down. This represents a positive transformation," says Rebecca. "It's a partnership between a local business and a developer wanting to do the best for a community. We wanted to demonstrate that change could be positive. The aim was to turn the space into a living, breathing thing." And so The Deptford Project was born.

"I've always felt fond of Deptford," says Rebecca, who grew up on one of the local estates. "There is a creative scene here. There are lots of start-up businesses, independent shops, and retailers and a really vibrant thrift market. It's culturally diverse and there's almost an untapped culture here. There are hidden treasures." Deptford High Street is a lively mix of discount stores, fast food and market stalls. For those seeking a moment of tranquillity, wander through the churchyard of St Paul's, the beautiful Baroque church. For performing arts, seek out The Albany on Douglas Way. Cross over New Cross Road at the southern end of the high street and you'll find a traditional family-run butcher's that's been going since 1829 and a modern Italian deli. There is even a pizzeria in a converted double-decker bus by Deptford Creek.

The Deptford Project tells the story of a vibrant area and of its regeneration that includes new housing, a shopping piazza and galleries. Rebecca has always wanted the café to be an investment for the community and for the people who work there. Some of the staff are students at

nearby Lewisham College and everyone who works at The Deptford Project café is as excited about being part of a unique venture as they are about food.

The railway carriage was rescued by Rebecca from a military airfield in Shoeburyness in Essex. At six months pregnant, she remembers clambering around a graveyard of carriages that were being used for target practice and destined to be blown-up. She selected the lucky carriage that was to be transformed into a café and set it off on a journey by road to London at a crawling pace of two miles per hour. On Valentine's Day 2008, the carriage arrived in Deptford as a present to the community, fittingly dubbed To Deptford With Love. By this time, Rebecca was the mother of a three-week old baby and the carriage was another significant arrival for her. "There was so much press coverage and pressure to keep up and maintain the project. I just got on with it," she says. The carriage was set onto rails and secured in its new home in the old railway yard.

Over the three months that followed the carriage was restored and transformed into the space you'll find today. The original seats were stripped out and the walls and ceiling were painted white. Small tables and chairs went into the long, narrow space, quirky light-fittings were hung from the low ceiling and a wooden dresser for self-service items such as water and sauces was set against a wall. The kitchen went in just two days before the carriage reopened its doors as a café. The carriage shell became a blank canvas on which artists were invited to make their mark. Every six months, a new artist will paint, stencil, or etch intricate designs onto the carriage to form a temporary exhibition.

Choosing to house the café in a converted train carriage was very much in keeping with the temporary feel of The Deptford Project. "Subliminally you get the notion it might move," says Rebecca. Yet the carriage has become a landmark in its own right, so much so that Cathedral Group included it in their plans for the whole site. In honor of the railway carriage, the new Richard Rogers-designed residential building in the development behind the railway yard has been christened The Carriage Building. Deptford might be changing but this old railway carriage from the 1960s is here to stay.

Look Mum No Hands!

49 Old Street, EC1V 9HX
020 7253 1025 www.lookmumnohands.com
Open: 7.30AM-10PM Mon to Fri, 9AM-10PM
Sat, 10AM-10PM Sun
Tube/rail: Old Street

LOOK MUM NO HANDS! is a café-bar-bike workshop set up by old friends and cyclists Sam Humpheson, Matt Harper and Lewin Chalkley. Before dreaming up their venture, Matt worked in banking. He was bored and dissatisfied, "the clichéd City worker." Sam, meanwhile, had acquired a reputation as a top bike mechanic, having worked for most of London's major bike shops. As for Lewin, he'd fallen into catering after college, then worked for Pret A Manger making sandwiches. He became involved in coffee and established a child-friendly café in Fulham, West London.

The friends knew there was a gap in the market for a café combined with a bike workshop that doubled as a venue for sports-related events. When Matt was made redundant from his City job, it was a case of now or never. "It was the perfect timing with Matt's redundancy," says Lewin. They started looking for a site. They knew they wanted somewhere with footfall and where lots of cyclists were passing. They settled on Old Street because it was one of the main arteries connecting East London with the West End and found a large site, a former architects' showroom with high ceilings. They spent two months transforming it into their venture and opened in April 2009.

Look Mum No Hands! soon became a fully-functioning café and bicycle workshop. It's a celebration of cycling with great food and drink on tap. Music plays out behind the conversation and the whirring of the coffee grinder. Customers perch on a row of stools along the bar facing the windows, sipping coffee and tapping away on laptops. The rest of the space is given over to tables and chairs, with more seating spilling out into the courtyard. Here, cyclists pause for a pit-stop, refuelling with a drink or a bite to eat and enjoy a breather from the buses and trucks which hurtle by. Call in for breakfast and you can tuck into free-range sausage and bacon sandwiches, muesli, and pastries. Lunch specialities are salad plates and homemade pies and on colder days there is soup and jacket potatoes with homemade beans. A friend's mum ("Auntie Liz") makes the cakes. Cool down with frappés, smoothies, and shakes, or go for a loose-leaf tea that's served in a little pot on a tray. And if you fancy something stronger there is an interesting range of ales and wine. Coffee is by Square Mile roasters. "The roaster of the moment," says Lewin. "And we have brilliant baristas."

Sam, Matt, and Lewin have created a space where cycling enthusiasts can come together to watch screenings and events organizers can host sports-related events. You'll find anything from book launches and presentations to the downright weird and wonderful, including world record-breaking cyclist James Bowthorpe (AKA the Nutter in the Window) who pedalled non-stop for 24 hours, the equivalent of 300 miles, in the café window as part of his training to cross the USA.

The location has proved even better than they had hoped for. If you pedal hard you can be on Oxford Street in ten minutes. With longer than average opening hours and an alcohol licence, it's easy to see why Look Mum No Hands! has become so popular with both the cycling and non-cycling locals. "We wanted to appeal to the broadest spectrum," says Lewin. Occasionally a well-behaved dog on a leash might trot in and, needless to say, no one will bat an eyelid if you wheel in a bike (if you've come without a bike lock just ask to borrow one). At weekends the Lycra-clad biking groups descend.

Bikes are displayed in the large windows looking out over Old Street and bike parts hang from the ceiling awaiting repair or assembly. The ceiling is decorated with colourful bunting and cycling items that are for sale. Posters and ads pinned to corkboards around a pillar are of a cycling theme, from tandem cycling tours to cycling clubs and bike polo.

The bike workshop is accessed via a door next to the counter, through which you can glimpse rows of tools hanging on the wall and a stack of work dockets spiked to the back of the door. A handful of bikes, awaiting attention or collection, spills out into the café. The emphasis is on high quality bike repairs. "It's the equivalent of Formula One cars in the bike world," Sam says. They also make a point of hiring female mechanics, too, so the workshop appeals to female customers as much as male.

People also go to Look Mum No Hands! for unique cycling-related gear. Matt, Lewin, and Sam launched their own range of branded accessories including cycling tops, caps, and bags that are available to buy in store or via their online shop. Stacked up around the coffee machine you'll find everything from quirky bike-lights and colourful tire levers to puncture repair kits in kooky little tins. Books and other cycling curios are displayed on shelves by the counter. You don't need to be a cycling fanatic to come here when the food and coffee are so good but if you are, you'll definitely feel at home.

Brunswick House Café

Brunswick House, 30 Wandsworth Road, Vauxhall SW8 2LG **020 7720 2926**
www.brunswickhousecafe.co.uk
Open: 8AM-5PM Mon, 8AM-11.30PM Tues to Fri, 10AM-11.30PM Sat, 10AM-5PM Sun
Tube/rail: Vauxhall

LOOK CLOSELY THROUGH THE GAPS in the traffic that thunders through the sprawling intersection of Vauxhall Cross in South London and you might spot Brunswick House. Dwarfed by high-rise glass towers, it's a Grade II Listed Georgian building that was built in 1758 as a home to the Dukes of Brunswick. It later fell into disrepair and became a rundown squat. Then in 2004, it was acquired and renovated by LASSCO

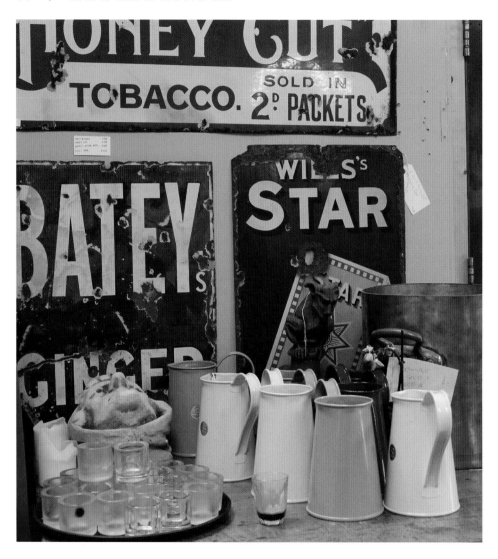

(The London Architectural Salvage and Supply Company).

Today Brunswick House is open to the public who come to browse through LASSCO's staggering collection of antiques and treasures from the past. Step inside and you'll be transported back in time through its vaulted cellar and warren of rooms that are crammed with curiosities from fireplaces and rugs to radiators and chandeliers. In one room sits a large Edwardian cast iron bath with original taps and plug. Walk through other rooms and you'll pass old signage from the London Underground, a row of 1950s cinema seats, brass door-knockers, and stacks of ceramic tiles. Everything is for sale. If you're after something weird or wonderful for your home, you'll find it here.

In 2010 a large storage annex on the ground floor of the house was given over to a café. It's a space large enough to seat 90 around an assortment of tables set beneath glittering chandeliers and lanterns. Huge mirrors, signs, and plaques line the walls and the floor is covered by a patchwork of rugs. Like everything else in the house, most items in this room are for sale. In the evening, the café turns into a restaurant and tea-lights twinkle on the tables. "I am completely in love with this," says Jackson Boxer, who set up the café with his younger brother Frank. "We can be a restaurant one night, a cinema the next. We've had film screenings here, too. I was quite clear about how I wanted it to look. It's a rather magnificent thing that's germinated from a seed of clarity thanks to the amazing staff and people here."

Jackson was just 25 when he and Frank established the Brunswick House Café. The brothers started up the café on a shoestring, spending their savings on the bare essentials. "I'm a great believer in just doing something," Jackson says. "We had a lot of confidence in what we were doing. I knew that if we took it seriously and worked really hard, we could do it." They set out to break down the conception that good food has to cost big bucks and created a menu that's simple yet brimming with flavours. It's food that's been created with love and care and the kind of cooking you'll remember for a long time after you've tasted it. For Jackson, good food isn't about being showy—it's about treating and seasoning the produce well. "It's about people taking time out of their day to sit down and enjoy something memorable. Life can be grey and humdrum, but a single well-made coffee, a platter of food, or a fresh lemonade creates a memory," he says.

Frank left Jackson at Brunswick House with an able team and went off to work on other projects (including running a bar on the roof of a multi-storey car park in Peckham). The first few months at the café were slow. "People would peer around the door, very amused," Jackson remembers. In the early days, they were a tiny operation in the front of the big room, serving espresso and simple salads. Fresh produce has always come from regular trips to New Covent Garden Market, the neighboring wholesale fruit and vegetable market. They deliberately avoid sandwiches as they can't compete on price with the corporate chains. "It's a menu that evolves daily. What the weather suggests and what we have in," says Jackson. "So it's very simple, nice lunchtime food. A café-style menu."

Every detail of the menu has been fine-tuned by Jackson and his team of chefs. Since the café opened they have outgrown the original kitchen and expanded into a larger room within this cavernous Aladdin's cave. 'It's thrilling, thrashing around ideas, experimenting with ingredients," says Jackson. There's the Blythburgh breakfast slider, described by Jackson as "a lovely shoulder and belly of pork, minced up, seasoned with thyme, cooked as burgers and served with savoury scones". For lunch, you might find wild garlic soup or venison terrine with toast and pickles. Go for dinner and kick-off with cocktails, dangerously potent little bombs of deliciousness that are not for the faint-hearted. The meat is a rare breed and the wines, which are sourced from small, specialist producers, are all marked up by the same amount to encourage customers to try some extraordinary wines at really good prices.

Vauxhall has never been particularly fashionable though there are pockets of wealth among the ramshackle and run-down quarters. There's a group of houseboats moored along the river and the area is home to mix of people from young families to students. A short walk away is Bonnington Square, a true bohemian corner of London, lined with eighteenth and nineteenth century houses that were famously squatted in the 1980s. Jackson grew up nearby and went to school around the corner from Brunswick House. "Since I was a kid I've always loved restaurants, cafés and bars," he says. He remembers his parents used to cook "with great love, using fresh vegetables, a bit of meat occasionally and quite a bit of offal." His grandmother is the cookery writer Arabella Boxer, a former contributor to the food pages of British Vogue

magazine for nearly 30 years. "She was incredibly influential to me," says Jackson. "Meals with her were always such a great treat, really grown-up."

Jackson has never advertised, choosing instead to rely on word-of-mouth. "When people discover a place for themselves, there's a romance to that, an investment," he says. Locals have come to depend on the café for everything from their morning pastries to leisurely lunches with colleagues. "You learn you have a place within a community," says Jackson. "Suddenly people are used to you being there. One morning we opened late as there was a mix-up and a customer was really indignant. I never expected that. I thought it was marvellous."

Now regulars call in for a coffee on their way to the station. "Everyone needs a good coffee," he says. And he's right, of course, but it seems wrong, somehow, to drop into Brunswick House Café for a single caffeine hit when the kitchen offers so much more. Go for lunch or book a table for dinner and fully indulge. This place is truly unique.

· 4 ·

NEIGHBOURHOOD GEMS

A NEIGHBOURHOOD CAFÉ can be a very special place. Ideally within strolling distance from your front door, it's about more than just the food and drink. It's a bolthole where the staff know your name, your coffee, and your favourite seat.

The best neighbourhood café is one that's open when you need it. It might open early or close late. Maybe it's open on a Sunday when everything else is closed and so it draws you in with its warm glow of familiarity. There might be local art on the wall, a stack of newspapers and magazines to browse through, and a resident cat or dog. It's a place where a community can come together and feel connected. Neighbors might meet for the first time and become friends over coffee. It's where a new parent might take his baby on its first outing and where that child will grow up.

Each visit may seem much the same as another but their accumulation can account for a significant part of our lives. When a neighbourhood café closes for a fortnight's holiday over Christmas or in the summer, its regulars will soon lament its absence. Whether your purpose for going is for conversation, food and drink, to work or just to switch off, the end result is the same—you'll feel better for having gone.

If you don't have a neighbourhood café to call your own, then the next best thing is to borrow someone else's. It may require more planning and a bus ride but going out of your way to get there can make the visit all the more memorable and open your eyes to a whole new neighbourhood.

TRY OUR
FRESH JUICES
OR HOW
ABOUT A
MILKSHAKE

Minkie's Deli

Glasshouse, Chamberlayne Road, Kensal Rise NW10 5RQ
020 8969 2182 www.minkiesdeli.co.uk
Open: 7.30AM-7PM Mon to Sat, 8AM-4PM Sun
Tube/Rail: Kensal Rise, Kensal Green

AS MANY AN ESTATE AGENT WILL ATTEST, the opening of a high street deli is often a sign that an area is on the up. As such, it would be fair to say that Kensal Rise came to life in 2007 when Minkie's Deli was opened by Doron Azmon and his wife Minkie. "Kensal Rise was not always deemed such a safe area. Years earlier people even quoted it as a crack den," says Minkie. "But Doron fell in love with the area. He saw the beauty in it."

Today the area is known to many as Media Rise, thanks to its proximity to White City—home to the BBC—and is a magnet for vibrant and creative people from actors and musicians to film directors and a sprinkling of celebrities including pop-stars and footballers. Its high-street's amenities are various—a post office, butcher, estate agents, off-license to name but a few—and the area's location on the northern fringe of central London is well served by public transport. Hop aboard one of the many buses that roll by and within minutes you'll be strolling down Portobello Road, London's famous antiques market in the heart of affluent Notting Hill. In a bid to escape the extortionate rents of Notting Hill, some of its fashionable boutiques have even started to creep northwards to Kensal Rise. The result? Property prices in Kensal Rise have gone through the roof.

So it's here, nearing the brow of the hill over Kensal Rise station that you'll find a greenhouse-like structure that is home to Minkie's, a deli and café. Next to the many tables and chairs arranged beneath the trees in the dappled sunlight you'll see an old market barrow laden with oranges for juicing. Step through the door, pull up a chair at one of the long wooden tables and be soothed by soft classical music. The many shelves are lined with jars, packets and tins of delicious delights to take home and a huge bunch of dried chillies hangs from a corner by the kitchen. Customers, writers perhaps, sit with their coffees, brainstorming or leafing through papers. A Kensal Rise celeb might pop in for a coffee knowing he won't be fussed over.

The small kitchen behind the counter is a hive of activity, from juicing and toasting to coffee and sandwich-making. There's another larger kitchen, out of sight, set into the hill beneath.

Today it's hard to imagine Kensal Rise without Minkie's. Yet, not long ago, the site where the café now stands housed a toilet block for bus drivers stationed at the depot at the foot of the hill. The block was knocked down and the land went up for auction. It was bought by an estate agent who constructed the glass shell of what was to become Minkie's. Doron and Minkie were desperate to turn it into a café-deli but when trying to raise finances, the banks they approached, sceptical of the prosperity of the area at that time, refused to lend to them. So they rallied round family

and friends and managed to raise enough funds to get Minkie's off the ground.

Doron, a former builder, tackled the entire fit-out himself from the plumbing and electrics, and turned the shell into the comfortable space it is today. Most of the furniture and fixtures are recycled relics that he had in storage from previous building contracts. The counter-tops and ledges around the windows were fashioned from old oak floor-boards and the homely wooden chest bearing tempting treats from Italian pastries to jars of cookie mix was rescued from an old plumber's workshop.

Doron and Minkie also own Brooks, the butcher's shop across the road, which they set up to operate in conjunction with Minkie's. Since opening, they've shifted the deli-side of the operation into Brooks, moving items such as cured meats and cheeses over there. In the summer, you can go to Brooks for a steak and take it back to Minkie's where they'll barbecue it for you under the trees. It's like being at home without having to do the washing up afterwards.

Born in Jerusalem to Moroccan and Austrian parents, it's hardly surprising that Doron's influences are eclectic. It was his mother, Victoria, who instilled in him a love of food and cooking. Now in her late 80s, she still visits from her Jerusalem home, setting up in Doron and Minkie's kitchen to share her culinary expertise. Doron recalls her Moroccan "cigars"—pastries, stuffed with spicy minced meat—and her Spanish omelettes that resemble mountains. "Twenty times better when she makes it," he says.

Choose from a tempting array of deli-style sandwiches, made to order while you wait, each one a brilliant marriage of flavours and a meal in itself. As colourful as their names, there's the Minx (salami, hummus, tahini, roast veggies, and greens), the Italian Job (cured meat, tomatoes, cheese, and greens) and the Too Nice (tuna, egg, and avocado).

Doron's award-winning salads (they won a gold medal at The Guild of Fine Food's Great Taste Awards) are renowned, too. "They're a fusion of Moroccan and Mediterranean with a bit of European," says Doron. At least twice a week, he makes nightly trips to New Covent Garden, London's wholesale fruit and vegetable market across the river in Vauxhall, returning with the best produce he can lay his hands on. By dawn, he'll be back in the kitchen at Minkie's with his sous-chef, preparing salads and cooking lasagnes and goulashes.

Some of the cakes are the kitchen's own creations, others are bought in from local suppliers. There are triple chocolate brownies, slices of peanut butter cheesecake, and cannolis—scrumptious Italian pastries arranged on gold plates, their crisp pastry shells bursting with chocolate and hazelnut cream. Minkie's is renowned for its full-flavoured coffee though Doron prefers to keep the identity of his roaster close to his chest. All he will say is that he works closely with him to develop the secret blend, a dark roast that's 100% arabica. Doron is very particular about his coffee. "When we go abroad, it's hell because he can never find a decent coffee," says Minkie.

When Minkie isn't working as a drama director for television (she directed popular off-beat comedy Skins), she's busy behind the scenes at the café. Though you won't find her at the stove. "I'm a terrible cook," she says. "I don't think I was born to be in the kitchen. It was a relief to meet Doron!"

Minkie's also does catering for private parties, bringing the deli to peoples' homes. "The presentation of food is very important to him," says Minkie, enthusing over the beautifully crafted platters her husband prepares. "He absolutely makes it a feast for the eyes as well. He uses all the senses." In the summer Minkie's will put together a picnic hamper to order, brimming with salads, cakes, and fruit, to pick up at an hour's notice. And for special occasions, such as Christmas and Valentine's Day, there are hampers, bursting with delicious goodies from mince-pies to pink Champagne.

At the café Doron seems to know everyone who walks through the door. You'll hear him greet all his customers, many by name. "He's always on his feet. It makes him tick, nurturing people through food. Being a host," says Minkie. He and Minkie live within walking distance to the café and can't get home without stopping and saying hello to people. Doron is known locally as the Mayor of Kensal. Whenever a problem arises in the community, often he's the first person people go to. When the council recently proposed relocating the bus depot outside Minkie's by demolishing the pavement and clearing the old trees in the process, Doron raised a petition and collected thousands of signatures. The development plans were scrapped.

Their customers have high expectations when it comes to the food, which is no bad thing, as you can be assured of the quality of everything that Doron sources. "They're real foodies round here," says Minkie. And he'll always go out of his way to produce an item for someone. A customer once wanted some proper rock salt, so Doron came to the rescue and tracked some down. He also

asked a friend to make some samples of wheat-free cakes for allergy-sufferers who frequent the café and Minkie's clementine cake was born. The personal connections are numerous. "Where we can, we support locals," says Minkie. Some of the wine they sell is made by the father of a local resident. It's all very community-driven. "People come away wanting more," says Minkie. "And I'm pretty sure that anyone who comes once comes back."

The Counter Café

7 Roach Road, Fish Island E3 2PA
07834 275 920 www.thecountercafe.co.uk
Open: 7.30AM-5PM Mon to Weds,
7.30AM-late Thurs to Fri,
8.30AM-late Sat, 8.30AM-5PM Sun
Tube/rail/DLR: Hackney Wick,
Pudding Mill DLR

I F THERE IS EVER A STORY that makes you want to quit your day job and set up your own business, Tom and Jess Seaton's is it. This brother-sister act is a firm believer in rolling up their sleeves, getting stuck in, and making things happen. "You've got to be willing to take a risk," says Jess. They grew up in Auckland and witnessed the explosion of New Zealand's café scene in the 1990s. Since then, they had a plan to open a café of their own and over the years that followed they built up scrapbooks of their plans and ideas. In 2003, they moved to the UK. "Six months turned into six years . . ." Jess says.

In terms of café culture, the UK was several years behind New Zealand. Tom was working for lager brand Stella Artois and could see that pubs were closing at an alarming rate. People's habits were changing and a shift seemed to be occurring. Was it perhaps a sign that the UK was ready for something new—more of a local community hub than pub? "There was a huge gap for it," Jess says. Tom was renting a place overlooking the Hertford Union Canal, in a far-flung corner of East London called Fish Island. The rent was cheap and he had converted part of the building into a living space. "The area was like tumbleweed but it was clearly the edgiest, most interesting and

arty," he says. In fact, this industrial wasteland has been credited with having one of the highest concentrations of artists in the world. Tom and Jess suggested opening a café in a vacant part of the building. The landlord agreed.

The moment The Counter opened in 2009, it immediately took off. The arts community had always been there but suddenly it had somewhere to come together. Neighbors who'd never met now had a space to socialise and relax. "All these people just popped out. They flocked here," says Jess. "We got incredible feedback from customers." The Counter became a place where friendships flourished and business relationships developed.

In recent years, the area has evolved and the community has widened. When construction work began across the canal on the Olympic Stadium for the London 2012 Olympic and Paralympic Games, Fish Island kicked into life. New flats went up and young professionals moved in. Jess and Tom's previous concerns about being off the beaten track turned out to be one of their café's key selling points. Thanks to food bloggers and reviews in the press, The Counter has become something of a food destination for gourmet tourists. Jess still remembers the group of people who kayaked down from Tottenham in North London specifically to visit.

In Spring 2011 The Counter moved out of its original site and relocated 20 metres down the road, sharing a space with exhibition and performance venue Stour Space. The café has retained its creative vibe, only now it's bigger and better. A tray of homemade brownies, biscuits and pastries still sits temptingly by the cash register. The floor is dotted with pot-plants and there are fresh flowers in jars on the tables. Like the old site, walls are bare brick or painted white and in places they've been knocked through—their unfinished edges are all part of the look. The row of old cinema seats has found a new wall to lean against. The coffee menu is chalked onto the wall among the art and posters advertising local events.

To create a new home for The Counter in the Stour Space, Jess and Tom remember sketching up designs, turning them into 3D models and sending them to the council's planning department for approval. Helped by local artists and residents, they labored into the early hours, knocking through walls to create more light and constructed huge windows that offer stunning views of the Olympic Stadium across the canal. They built the galley kitchen in an old fire-escape alleyway.

Six-times the size of the kitchen in the old site, it has space for up to 15 cooks. And they designed a sizeable deck out onto the canal, that makes a perfect spot for soaking up rays.

Like most of the staff who work in the kitchen, Jess and Tom have had no formal chef training, "We're just a very foodie family. Our mother is a culinary genius," says Jess. They describe the menu as "all-day gourmet brunch". It's substantial, tasty, and made from the best quality ingredients they can get hold of. They now stay open into the evening to serve tapas-style food and sharing plates matched with wine.

Fresh produce comes from Organic Wick, a veg-box scheme that's run by local volunteers and enables them to offer the best ingredients at normal prices. To this day they'd still be making regular trips to the supermarket for a brand of eggs renowned for their orange yolks and rich flavour had the egg company not started delivering. Eggs are served any style with homemade potato cakes and little dishes of house chutney on the side (also for sale by the jar). Their pies are their own recipes—"we just made them up," says Jess—and include a lamb, eggplant, and lentil pie with a crunchy mint and onion topping and a mince and cheese pie that's wrapped in flaky golden pastry. "Pies are a massive Kiwi thing," says Jess. "We've totally ramped it up to a whole new level." If they can make it themselves, they will. They went to France to learn how to make croissants in a *boulangerie* with Marie, who is French and runs the prep kitchen. They now bake some of their bread and pastries.

Coffee has always been from Square Mile roasters. "They're freakishly geeky about coffee," says Jess. She trains all the baristas herself and ensures they're up to scratch before they're let loose on the espresso machine. As for the staff, the main criteria is that they get along with the rest of the team and are willing to learn on the job. "A lot are New Zealanders or Scandinavians and are away from home," says Jess. "We've built it into a real family." There's a real sense of helping each other out. "It's win-win," says Tom. "Everyone gets something out of it."

Every time you return to The Counter it's likely that you'll find they have a new project in the pipeline. It's the kind of place that's constantly evolving. "We want this to be a long-term sustainable business," says Tom. They hold cinema and acoustic nights and they've even hosted a music festival. Every last Saturday of the month in the main gallery there's a Designer Makers Market, where local independent makers and artists sell their wares. And in 2012, the Seatons opened a micro-brewery and pizza bar in nearby Hackney Wick.

If you fancy walking off your breakfast, take a stroll along the Greenway—a seven-kilometre raised walkway that stretches through East London—to check out The Counter's sister café, The Container. You'll find it in the View Tube, a social enterprise housing an information, arts, and education space. Situated moments from the Olympic Park and constructed from bright green shipping containers, it's hard to miss. The Container caters more for families, walking groups and passers-by and you'll find equally good coffee and food here. But it's at The Counter Café that you'll linger with the weekend papers and feel inclined to order a third coffee.

Tina, We Salute You

47 King Henry's Walk, Dalston N1 4NH
020 3119 0047 www.tinawesaluteyou.com
Open: 8AM-5PM Mon, 8AM-7PM Tues to Fri,
8AM-7PM Sat, 10AM-7PM Sun
Tube/rail: Dalston Junction,
Dalston Kingsland

PROBABLY ONE OF THE MOST origi-nal names for a café, the Tina of Tina, We Salute You is the woman depicted in the famous 1960s painting by British artist J. H. Lynch who was renowned for his por-traits of sultry women. Steve Hawkes and his partner Danny Hilton were running a cupcake stall on Sundays in London's Brick Lane market at the time they bought the Tina print on eBay. "It was retro and naff, so we hung her on the stall," Steve says. One evening, over too much red wine, they came up Tina, We Salute You for the name for their cupcake stall. "We were drunk and it was the first name we thought of!" he laughs.

They ran the stall for a year-and-a-half until the idea of opening a café started to take hold. They knew what they wanted in a café—a space where people could chill out for an hour or so with excellent coffee and freshly made food. Steve had spent a couple of years in Australia and had been inspired by the Antipodean café scene. They decided to open a place in East London, their home turf. "I've lived in Dalston forever," says Steve. The site on King Henry's Walk had been empty for over 10 years. It was a few minutes by bike from their home and its corner

position was perfect for a café. They packed up Tina and moved in. They reframed her (they found a frame in the street and cut the print to fit) and hung Tina in her new home. "We knew we wanted Tina," Steve says.

You'll find Tina, We Salute You a few minutes' walk away from the commercial chaos of Dalston's main thoroughfare, the Kingsland Road. Tucked down a quiet backstreet, it's a residential area with a church across the road, a betting shop and a pub on the other corner. That it's on the cusp of three postcodes (E8, N1, and N16) is neither here nor there—the café is definitely Dalston and known to its many devotees simply as Tina's.

The extended East London Overground that connects Dalston Kingsland and Junction stations to the Olympic Village in Stratford, the southern reaches of Croydon and Richmond in the West, has put Dalston firmly on the map. "Dalston was recently described as the epicentre of cool!" Steve laughs. The Kingsland Road, which stretches from Shoreditch to Stoke Newington, is a colourful mishmash of fast food outlets, minicab offices, and pound shops (there's even a 98p shop). And directly opposite Dalston Kingsland station you'll find Ridley Road market, a vibrant blend of Afro-Caribbean, West Indian, Turkish, and Greek where reggae music blasts across the stalls which sell fabrics, household goods, and fruit and vegetables at bargain basement prices.

The look that Steve and Danny wanted for the café was retro and dated—a bit like Tina. Hence the beaten-up old sofa, moulded plastic school-style chairs, the 1970s pull-down lights and the rocking chair. "The communal table was a bit traumatic for some people at first," Steve smiles, remembering how most customers were used to having their own table, "but people are fine with it now." Come mid-morning, the table bears evidence of shared breakfasts—toast crumbs and jars of marmite and jams—and other tables spill out onto the pavement and up the side of the café where people bake in the sun, gossip and smoke.

Their natural flair for baking is evident in Danny's carrot and banana cakes; the upside-down pineapple cake; a truly amazing salted caramel tart; and, of course, cupcakes. Almond croissants are provided by a friend who runs a bakery in Stoke Newington and they buy all their fruit and vegetables from a local grocer's.

Coffee is provided by East London roasters

Square Mile. Steve and Danny regularly make the coffee themselves and have always made a point of hiring really good baristas. As well as being a true local gem, the coffee at Tina's—full-flavoured shots with perfectly steamed milk—is consistently excellent. As for the sandwiches, the term doorstopper must surely have been invented here. Two hunks of bread, made to order, contain combinations of ham from Brindisa, cheese from Neal's Yard Dairy and relishes and fresh leaves.

While away a morning at Tina's and you'll witness a whole range of locals coming and going, popping in on their own or with friends and family. "We get a lot of locals. There are huge regulars," Steve says. There are a lot of creative types, artists, and designers, who chain their pushbikes to the stands outside. On weekdays, mums wheel in toddlers and families drop by on weekends. Children sit in the window devouring cupcakes and playing board-games next to a pile of weekend newspapers for their parents. Almost everyone seems to know the staff or each other. It's the kind of place where people take their empty cups back to the counter when they pay and the music is loud enough to hum along to without detracting from the conversation.

The art in Tina's is as key to the café as the food and drink. Every eight weeks, the walls are whitewashed and a local artist is invited to decorate the café. Any medium goes. One Christmas Steve and Danny decided to decorate the café themselves and created the wonderfully camp '70s Christmas Lounge. They hung gaudy retro wallpaper, installed a seven-foot wicker palm tree complete with coconut lamps, fairy lights and lots of tinsel. "The art's really big. It's got a life of its own," Steve says. "We never wanted anything in frames—it's straight onto the wall. There's nothing we'd refuse. We give the artists a set of keys and they come in when we're closed. We might whiz past at night and have a peek," he says. The work is exhibited for the following eight weeks, then the process starts again.

Steve and Danny have organized various events and pop-up nights at Tina's. Once, the café was transformed into a speakeasy for ten nights complete with blacked-out windows, a special telephone number for booking, and passworded entry. Even Tina joined in the fun by sporting a blindfold. The plan is to find another backstreet location where they can set up a full-time bar and host evening events and the current Tina's can focus on being a wonderful neighbourhood café.

Fernandez & Wells

73 Beak Street, Soho W1F 9SR
020 7287 8124 www.fernandezandwells.com
Open: 7.30AM-6PM Mon to Fri,
9AM-6PM Sat, 9AM-5PM Sun
Tube: Piccadilly Circus, Oxford Circus,
Tottenham Court Road

THE MEETING of Jorge Fernandez and Rick Wells came about in 2005, or thereabouts. Rick was working as a presenter on BBC World Service radio at Bush House in Aldwych and used to stop off in Monmouth Coffee in Covent Garden where Jorge was manager. The pair became acquainted and in 2006 they quit their day jobs and went into business together. "I was interested in food and wine and I quite liked the idea of running a small business," says Rick. "We spent the best part of six months making a plan, walking the streets of London, looking, talking and formulating ideas. We thought we'd combine our interests while keeping it really simple, both in the look as well as the offering."

Soho seemed like a good foodie location and the site they found in Lexington Street— a former clothing boutique—just felt right. They wanted it to be like a market-stall in feel, where you drop by off the street. As their designs came together they started to worry that space was becoming too tight to include a coffee machine on the counter. By chance there was another shop site for rent in a similar early Georgian townhouse just around the corner on Beak Street.

So they converted the ground floor into a café selling coffees and sandwiches, using the same builders to achieve a similar look across both sites. The paving stones on the floor in Lexington Street were used to create the café counter in Beak Street. They opened the Brit-European food and wine bar in Lexington Street and the Beak Street café early in 2007 and now the two sites play off each other. You can buy a coffee in Beak Street and drink it in the bar in Lexington Street if, say, you're with a friend who fancies a glass of wine.

Make sure you're hungry before you step into Beak Street. If you're not already smitten by the smell of coffee, then the colourful sandwiches and tempting cakes on the counter beg to be devoured. The food is fresh and simple. "If we ever started to get carried away, we thought of a shepherd and what he might take as a packed lunch in his knapsack. That was our guiding principle," says Rick. "So it was bread, cheese, cured meats, wine, and coffee as the starting point. We make very little. It's just preparation and putting them out fresh. We wanted to keep that feel of a market. We make it and off it goes."

They realized that what they were good at was hunting down suppliers and selecting quality products. "Customers seem to trust us," says Rick. The bread is traditional stone-baked baguettes and ciabatta-style buns and an Irish lady called Bee makes their cakes. She insisted on using their espresso in her coffee and walnut cake. Sandwich fillings are combinations of fresh and cured meats (grilled chorizo, rare roast beef, and Dorset ham, for example) and cheese, including Montgomery's cheddar from Somerset and Spanish Manchego, teamed with salad, mustards, and tangy chutneys.

In 2009 Rick and Jorge opened a third site in Soho's St Anne's Court, a pedestrian alleyway connecting nearby Wardour Street and Dean Street. "It was a bit of a risk. It's not an obvious site, a typical seedy Soho alley," says Rick. It's an espresso bar with some elements of food and wine and it's open in the evening.

Rick sources the wines and oversees the administration, licensing and leases. Jorge looks after the operational side of things. Sometimes you might see him behind the counter with an apron on. "Where we come together is the food, the products," says Rick. "And we do the rounds between the three shops."

Fernandez & Wells has a loyal following. At busy times, the Beak Street café can be bursting at the seams. Grab one of the little stools, if you can, and tuck yourself into a perch along the wall or in the window. It's Soho, so you'll find people from fashion, media, advertising, film production and the rag trade. "It's such a good mix here," says Rick. "There's young, old, relaxed and the cool crowd. Plus we're a stone's throw from Regent, Oxford and Carnaby Streets, so at the weekends there's the shoppers and tourists. People sniffing out a good coffee."

Lantana

13 Charlotte Place, Fitzrovia W1T 1SN
020 7637 3347 www.lantanacafe.co.uk
Open (Lantana IN): 9AM-6PM Mon to Fri,
9AM-5PM Sat and Sun
Tube: Goodge Street, Tottenham Court Road

SHELAGH RYAN REMEMBERS CLEARLY the day she opened the doors to her café Lantana. "It was nerve-wracking," she says. Hoping for a soft opening without any PR, she had spread the word via family and friends. "It was 25 September 2008, a clear blue day. This man walked in and had poached egg on toast." The following two weeks were pretty quiet, then the café was reviewed in London's weekly magazine Time Out and suddenly everything went crazy. In fact, the café became so popular that in April 2010 Shelagh expanded into the unit next-door, converting it into a takeout-only version of the café to ease congestion in the original space. So now you'll find two Lantanas—an In and an Out—that work in harmony with each other.

The café is tucked down a quiet passageway near Charlotte Street, known for its bars, restaurants, and eponymous hotel. This is Fitzrovia, the central London neighborhood just north of Soho and moments from bustling Tottenham Court Road. Nearby on Cleveland Street, one of London's tallest landmarks, the BT Tower, casts its shadow over neighboring buildings.

Lantana takes its name from the plant that was introduced to Australia from South America. "It's an iconic Australian plant. Actually it's a weed," says Shelagh, who is Australian herself.

"We liked the metaphor. It's as if we will get into the native flora and fauna. It's also known as the ham and egg plant. That did it for me!"

Lantana has a loyal following and its menu extends beyond cold sandwiches and salads. "I'd describe it as modern Australian," Shelagh says. "It's fusion cuisine using the best quality ingredients." Breakfast favorites include toasted banana bread with compote and their scrambled egg is so deliciously buttery you'll need a serviette to mop your face with afterwards. Arrive at midday and breakfast will have rolled into the lunch menu. Here you'll find much loved dishes including corn fritters with crispy bacon, freshly made tarts and a sandwich called The Bert (bacon, egg, rocket, and tomato). Drinks include beer and wine from Italy to New Zealand, pots of loose-leaf tea, and expertly made coffee. And a selection of baked and sweet treats include friands, the little oval almond cakes that are so much a part of cafés in Australia.

Shelagh first discovered Australia's café culture in Melbourne. "I felt I'd really found home in

the markets and the food scene," she says. On the advice of her sister Caitlin, who was living in London, Shelagh came over for a three-week recce in October 2007. Back home in Australia, she spent the following year up wading through research and devising a business plan, a concept and a menu.

The following year she moved to London and started looking for a site. "I hopped on my bike and went all over London," she says. "The brunch market wasn't as developed here as in Australia and we needed to go somewhere central with footfall," she says. She focussed her search on central London. Fitzrovia appealed as it was full of her ideal customers—those seeking something a bit quirky and an alternative to chains.

Yet her search proved a frustrating process. Sites would fall through and the financial downturn hit. Just as she began to wonder what she was doing, she found the site on Charlotte Place. It was a former Turkish restaurant and she loved it instantly. "It was spot-on," she says. "Just as we were going through the final negotiating, the papers announced that the markets were collapsing. I felt sick in the climate we were opening in," she recalls. "We opened right at the beginning of it though it's actually been a blessing as we've not known anything different."

Her sister Caitlin and brother-in-law Michael invested in the business too. Over the course of eight weeks, they gutted the site and moved the kitchen downstairs. "I thought, if we're going to do this, let's do it properly," Shelagh says. They installed a large window at the front that opens fully to connect with the outdoors, a typical feature of many Australian cafés. She commissioned Australian artist Kat Macleod to design the striking mural for the back wall and had it tailor-made into wallpaper to fit the space. It's also a key feature of their website.

Weekday customers are local professionals from creative industries—TV, film, advertising, post-production, and design agencies—who pile into Lantana to catch up over coffee or lunch. At weekends people travel from further afield, seeking refuge in laid-back Lantana away from the nearby madness of London's best-known busy shopping districts. It's easy to see why many of Lantana's regulars are Australian. Other cafés might pop up nearby but Shelagh's not fazed by new competition. "We're raising the bar and bringing people to the area," she says. Go to Lantana and you'll soon see why.

Munson's Coffee & Eats Co.

73 St Mary's Road, Ealing W5 5RG
020 8840 4114 www.munsons.co.uk
Open: 7AM-6PM Mon to Fri, 8AM-6PM Sat and Sun
Tube/rail: South Ealing, Ealing Broadway

YOU CAN SMELL THE COFFEE as you make your way down St Mary's Road towards Munson's. "It's our own cologne called coffee," smiles Panayiotis Sinnos (Panos) who helps to run the café with his cousins Marios and Pan Papacosta. Their brother Abraham works there every week, as does their cousin Neoklis. Even Panos's two nieces, Stella and Antigone (Tiggy), have pulled their share of shifts behind the counter. And then there is Andreas

Papacosta, father to Marios, Pan and Abraham, who oversees the whole operation and is affectionately known as The Godfather.

The family is from Cyprus and has always been in the catering industry, running fish and chip shops since the early 1960s. "There's this work ethic that comes from our family," says Panos. "I don't think any of us has been out of work ever. It's not difficult what we do but it's hard. You squeeze in a day-and-a-half's work into one day. I've become a bit of a workaholic. I just can't stop!"

Munson's location, away from Ealing's main shopping strip, has been part of the café's success. It's a creative area with residents that include holistic practitioners and landscape gardeners. Ealing Studios—the oldest television and film production company in the world—is based just down the road, so there's a lot of location shooting. Even at 8 o'clock on a Sunday morning you'll find staff buzzing around the café and customers popping in and out. "Being here has meant we've got to know the locals," says Panos. "It's easy for people to call in and it's not as noisy as the main high street. We've introduced people to their neighbours. Plus I think we all met our partners here. We've got a hardcore base of customers who've become our friends."

The story behind the café's name is somewhat convoluted. The name Munson comes from the 1950s in Cyprus where a family relative had a cat called Thurman and a dog called Munson after the New York Yankees player, Thurman Munson. So the café is named after a golden Labrador.

When Pan opened Munson's in 1998 it was in the site next-door (which Pan has since converted into a frozen yogurt store called Finster's, after Howard Finster, the outsider artist). Back then, the area was much quieter. "Pan found his niche on his own. He just did coffee and had three tables and six chairs," Panos says, who quit his banking career to join him. The café took off and ten years later they moved to the larger corner site at number 73, in what was supposed to be a temporary move for six months while they carried out refurbishments. The customers flocked in. "We got hit hard!" remembers Panos. "And here we still are. I think our secret has always been to run it as if we were having a party at home. If anyone's misbehaving we'll tell them how it is. Plus we always said that we've got to do good coffee… Coffee's the thing we do. Lord knows how many I've made over the years. Close to half a million, I'd imagine!" They do a small latté in a glass, like a piccolo or Spanish cortado. "Cortado sounds like "frog" in Greek," says Panos.

"So we call it a Frog on the menu. Customers come in now and they'll ask for a Frog."

As for food, there are sandwiches and a selection of large, sticky pastries and fresh bakes. Everything's made on site. The sandwich fillings change every day and always contain an extra little something—a relish, a mustard, or marmalade. The key to the menu, Marios says, is its simplicity. Marios's mother Georgina and Neoklis's mother Evangelia do the baking. The chocolate cookie cake and the zucchini and almond cake are their two most popular creations. It's cash-only, there's no Wi-Fi, and the music is a big part of the atmosphere. "Gangster rap to Debussy and everything in between," says Marios. "Though often it's something nostalgic you might not have heard for a while."

Munson's even opens on Christmas Day. "We have a band playing and we don't charge anyone," says Marios. Instead, customers are asked to leave a donation, if they wish, in a box and all the money is given to a local charity or school. It's all part of the strong community ties that are so important to Marios, Panos, and the team.

"In the old site, there was an intimacy. It was so small, you couldn't hide," says Panos. "But people still have to engage with us here. In the early days we didn't even label our sandwiches, deliberately so people would have to ask us what was in them. There was no grabbing, giving your money and leaving!" There are plenty of tables and chairs in this homely corner site, both inside and out the front. Walk down the step past the counter and you'll find a room with more tables and chairs tucked away out of sight. The art on the walls is for sale. Most of the photography is Panos's—you can see his portfolio on the website—the oil paintings are by Abraham and Neoklis and some of the acrylics were painted by Panos's wife Debra.

Before it became a café, the site was a bicycle shop for 40 years. Before that, it was a bakers. Step outside, look closely at the side of the building and, faded into the brickwork, you can just about make out the last three letters of the word Hovis, an old advert for the famous bakers. "Back in those days it was said that when it snowed, the snow would always melt on the pavement at the front of the shop, as the ovens were directly beneath," says Marios.

Petitou

63 Choumert Road, Peckham SE15 4AR
020 7639 2613 www.petitou.co.uk
Open: 9AM-5.30PM Mon to Sat,
10AM-5.30PM Sun
Rail: Peckham Rye

STROLL AWAY from Peckham's main drag, and on the edge of a conservation area nestled among handsome Victorian terraces, you'll stumble upon Petitou. A chalkboard menu promising "tea, coffee, hot and cold food to takeout, and nice things for your pantry" is propped up against a huge tree, a London Plane, and there's a scattering of tables and chairs on the terrace. You might imagine this handsome corner site has been a café forever but the building started life as a butcher's and dairy in the 1850s. It then became a hairdressers then, after a derelict spell, it reopened as a café. Today it's owned by Clare and Matt Bloxidge and it's hard to walk past without being drawn in.

Clare and Matt met over twenty years ago in Greece where they worked in bars and on yachts. After returning to London, Clare quit her City job and, seeking adventure, sailed to Antigua in the Caribbean with Matt and a friend. After a few years of working on yachts and managing a bar, Clare and Matt hatched a plot to open a café. They had a wish list: somewhere quirky

with outside space, a mishmash of furniture, artwork, and wooden floors. The day they returned to London, Clare's older sister Lorraine, a ceramic artist, tipped Clare off about a former café that was for sale in Peckham. Lorraine had been commissioned to design its terrace as a world map and had suggested that a map of Peckham, using coloured tiles to depict roads, railway lines and other key landmarks, would be more fitting for a local café. At the time, the South-East London suburb was being regenerated and local businesses were given council grants to improve their facades by involving artists—hence the terrace commission. The moment Clare and Matt saw the space, they knew it ticked all their boxes. In July 2003, they got the keys and another adventure began.

They thought it would be a two-week job to get their café up and running—it ended up taking two months. "It was so run down. It hadn't been trading for months so we had to gut it, rewire it and start from scratch," says Clare. "It was a really hot summer. We were painting, sanding, varnishing… Then we had to decide on a menu and suppliers. It was a huge learning curve. There were no accounts so we had to build our reputation from nothing." As for the furniture, some was inherited and the rest Clare found in junk shops and antique markets. They installed wooden booths and freestanding tables—most of them are now dotted with bottles of brown sauce and ketchup—and a homely coat-stand. Clare's brother-in-law Stephen, a carpenter, made two stools and a large table from old floorboards.

Clare and Matt used leftover money from the council grant to enlist Lorraine and local metal-worker Andy Grant to design and make the planters for the terrace. Andy also designed the security gates around the doors. They kept the café's original name from its previous owner who had named it after a beach in the Caribbean. In October, a brand new Petitou opened and their first day's takings of one hundred and seventy pounds were more than they'd hoped for.

Today Petitou is very much part of the local community. Leaflets for local business and events are scattered around windowsills, there's a notice-board for ads and local artists exhibit work on the walls. Instead of laptops you're more likely to see strollers, highchairs, and children's books and instead of music you'll hear conversation. Clare and Matt now have two children of their own. "We see the cycles of life," says Clare. "From a customer who's pregnant, then brings the baby in on its first visit. Before you know it, they're off to school." Customers come from all walks of life. You might share a table with a policeman sipping a milkshake, a student engrossed in a book, or an artist discussing a new project. The small galley kitchen is on full view and a door behind the counter opens onto the side street from where you can order food and drink to take away if you don't have time to sit.

The small kitchen means that Clare and Matt have to be inventive with the menu. Breakfast is served all day (pastries, eggs, muesli) and for lunch there are sandwiches, salads, quiches, and soup in winter. "We have four local ladies who make amazing cakes for us. And the previous owner's mum makes the quiches," says Clare. The tea and coffee is Fairtrade and organic and coffee beans come from Coffee Plant who roast to order. The blend has remained the same since they opened as customers love it. And to take home, you'll find all sorts of goodies from homemade chutneys and herbal teas to olive oil, nuts, and chocolates.

Sometimes Petitou is hired out for events. It's been used as a wedding reception venue and as a location for short films and magazine shoots. And every December Clare and Matt host a weekly Christmas Fair, where local artists hire tables and sell their wares. Leafy Choumert Road and its surrounding area have a strong artistic history. Many of the people who work at Petitou are students at nearby Camberwell College of Arts.

Clare and Matt's friend Olivia Colman is an actor who lives a couple of roads away. She comes in most days for coffee and cake or scrambled eggs, either to read through scripts or with her

children for mini-hot chocolates. "Petitou is the centre of our universe and Clare and Matt are just heavenly," she says. "You get a lot of writers, actors and musicians around here. You'll see people making jewellery at tables. There's a gentleness to the area. It's just that sort of place. Things have collided to make this café so lovely. It's like an extension of your sitting room."

Then there's Ann Winn who lives next-door to Clare and Matt on Choumert Road. She's a retired teacher and painter who trained at the Slade—the prestigious School of Fine Art—and now paints from the studio at the bottom of her garden. She comes to Petitou most days and recalls the first time she came to Choumert Road: "I walked up Rye Lane and came down the side street. There were so many trees. I fell in love with the street and the complexity of the people who lived here." She moved into the road in 2003 just as Clare and Matt were getting the café up and running. Ann was taken by the care they were putting into the finer details and when the café opened it soon became a focal point for her. "They do a very nice line in crumpets and thick toast. The home-cooking's wicked and they do a pretty mean scrambled eggs. There's soup in winter—not your junk stuff either, they start from scratch," she says. "Clare and Matt are keen on getting people together. I do on occasion come here every day. It's tremendously social."

Loyal regulars Don Weniz and partner Sandra Knight live a couple of streets away. They moved here in 1993 because they had friends in the area and liked the community feel. They remember when Petitou opened and come regularly for breakfast, lunch, or just coffee. "Right from the beginning it made an impact," Don says. "It's an incredibly friendly area, almost like a village. Matt and Clare are the sweethearts of the neighbourhood in many ways." Andy Stuart, one of their friends, is partial to Petitou's crumpets with peanut butter, jam, and cheese. "A lot of people won't entertain it," he says, "but they'll do it here." He brings his dog Maddie, an English Springer, and usually orders from the side door.

Now their children are older, Clare and Matt have been able to refocus on the business. They still share the café shifts, so one of them is usually at the café, and between them they continue to be very hands-on with their customers. The residents of Choumert Road are really very lucky indeed.

Queen's Wood Café

**Queen's Lodge, 42 Muswell Hill Road,
Highgate** N10 3JP
020 8444 2604 www.queenswoodcafe.co.uk
Open: 10AM-5PM **Mon to Sun**
Tube: Highgate

TAKE THE NORTHERN LINE up to Highgate in the London Borough of Haringey and in scarcely half an hour you'll be transported from the bustle of central London to what feels like the countryside. Climb the steps from the Tube up to street level and you'll suddenly be surrounded by trees. A short walk through the woods down Muswell Hill Road will take you to a white signpost that's marked simply Café. Go through the gate here, into the woods, and you'll see Queen's Wood Café. From the café veranda, looking out through the shady canopies of the trees, you'll hear birds singing. You might see a speckled wood butterfly or a squirrel scampering away. And every so often the sounds of nature are punctuated by a bus chugging by out of sight, a dog barking, or a lawn being mowed.

"I found romance late in life," says Murray Shelmerdine, who owns Queen's Wood Café. "My lovely wife Wanjiku and I were walking through Queen's Wood and saw this wonderful building, derelict. We were terribly interested in ecology and I happened to have a bit of money

in my pocket." Keen to turn the site into an eco project and to restore the building, the couple made some enquires. They discovered that the lodge had originally been built as a wood-keeper's cottage and that Haringey Council could not afford to renovate it. Neither was the council allowed to knock it down because of a dedication made in 1898 by the Duchess of Albany stating that it would be "for the use and enjoyment of the public forever." You can read it on a plaque on the wall of the lodge.

Happily Murray and Wanjiku were awarded a grant to restore the building and the garden. They rebuilt the veranda with oak from sustainable forests in Devon and Cornwall, then tackled the roof, the dry rot, and the rising damp. They scrubbed off the graffiti. Then they moved in because no one would insure the building unless someone was resident. And so in April 1998, one of the

wettest Aprils on record, they lived among the building work. "We had no heating, no shower, no kitchen. We had buckets to catch the drips," remembers Murray. "We lived like this for several weeks, months even." Meanwhile a handful of volunteers started work on the garden, putting down new compost and soil. They were the first building in Haringey to have solar panels. "On a good, sunny day, we probably run our lighting and computers from them," says Murray.

In the Spring of 1999, Murray and Wanjiku officially opened Queen's Wood Café. It started out as a vegetarian and organic café that was just open on weekends. "Though we couldn't sustain the organic side of it," says Murray. "And we weren't making enough money being vegetarian." So they expanded the menu and the opening hours. Now the café is open every day of the week. The menu is far-ranging and mostly everything is homemade on site. There are cooked breakfasts, soups, salads, pastas, pizzas, and toasted ciabattas. Those with a sweeter tooth can enjoy carrot cake, chocolate cake, and polenta cake with berries and you can share a jug of Pimms on the veranda.

Visitors to the café are invited to wander round the garden. "I am absolutely hopeless in the garden. I freely admit that," says Murray. "We have a regular gardener called Gillian." They keep bees in hives and sell honey by the jar. "We can't make enough of it," he says. "A lovely lady called Liz looks after the bees. I go and talk nicely to them from time to time." And for younger visitors, they installed a jungle walkway next to the lodge where children can work off their energy.

In the garden there's an ancient apple tree and a damson tree and they grow gooseberries, strawberries, raspberries, cabbages, and chives. "And pansies which are awfully nice in salads when they're in season," says Murray. "It's all in relatively small quantities but it's like a kitchen garden." There's also a little pond—they're hoping for frogs and more amphibian life—and they compost kitchen waste and dead leaves. "We're very into composting. We encourage people to pee on it to help it along," says Murray.

Queen's Wood, one of the four ancient woods in Haringey, was named after Queen Victoria in 1898 and was declared a Nature Reserve in 1990. The woods are ancient oak-hornbeam and are believed to be a direct descendent of the original wildwood that covered much of Britain thousands of years ago. There are also wild service trees, a native broadleaf tree whose berries have been used as a remedy for colic and in beer-making. The small river running through the woods, the Mosel, lends its name to nearby Muswell Hill. The woods attract a wide variety of birds including blue tits, wrens, and woodpeckers. Some even nest in the lodge's eaves. The woods are steeped in history and are still used by witches. During Midsummer Solstice and Halloween pagans gather in a glade surrounded by thirteen oak trees along the path from the café.

The café's core customers are mothers with children and dog-walkers who sit out on the veranda. On weekends crowds descend both inside and out. The café is used by a weekly writers' group and a poetry and music group once a month. Art is exhibited on the walls. Another specialty is children's themed parties that Murray runs, from pirates and fairies to Peter Pan. "We take the children on a wonderful adventure through the woods, every weekend in the summer. Oh yes, we have fairies at the bottom of the garden," Murray says with a wink.

ScooterCaffè

132 Lower Marsh, Waterloo SE1 7AE
020 7620 1421
Open: 8.30AM-11PM Mon to Thurs,
8.30AM-midnight Fri to Sat, noon-10PM Sun
Tube/rail: Lambeth North, Waterloo,
Waterloo East

STUMBLE ALONG LOWER MARSH and into ScooterCaffè on a cold, bleary morning and you'll soon start to warm up. Pendant lights with pink-tinged bulbs hang from the ceiling and the room takes on a greenish glow from the flourescent *Caffè* sign hanging near the bar. Resident cats snuggle down in comfy chairs around the room and the shelf behind the bar is lined with an impressive collection of old espresso machines.

Despite being a short skip from the river Thames, Lower Marsh is surprisingly understated. Linking Westminster Bridge Road with Waterloo Road, it seems to be one of London's forgotten streets. Tourists who flock to nearby attractions along the Southbank, such as the London Eye ferris wheel or the Royal Festival Hall, may skirt the edges of Lower Marsh without ever knowing it exists.

Yet venture off the beaten track and into this quiet, unassuming road behind Waterloo Station and you'll find an assortment of amenities. There are a few small chains, a couple of vintage clothing boutiques and a handful of bars and everyday cafés. For over 150 years Lower Marsh,

so-called because it was built on the drained marshland of ancient Lambeth Marsh, has been home to a street market. In recent years, though, only a few stalls remain. The white outlines painted on the road depicting the pitches remain as a reminder of the stalls that were once there. Developers have edged in and rents have soared. There is even talk of pedestrianising Lower Marsh and lining it with trees. As you make your way past the crêpe stall and Thai restaurant and takeaway you might notice the same song playing on the radio from market stall to shop, the airwaves zig-zagging across the road. During quiet moments, shop-owners stand in doorways, smoking and talking.

As Lower Marsh crosses Westminster Bridge Road it becomes Upper Marsh and twists

towards the Thames. It's at this end of Lower Marsh, where trains scrape over the bridge in and out of Waterloo station, that you'll find ScooterCaffè. Its owner Craig O'Dwyer likes Lower Marsh because it's nice and quiet and he knows mostly everyone on his end of the street. "Everyone keeps an eye on everyone else," he says.

When Craig and his former business partner bought the four-storey building in the late 1990s it was a crack-house and inhabited by squatters. There was no glass in the windows. They converted the ground-floor into a scooter workshop business with a sideline in repairing espresso machines. The espresso machine repair business never really took off—Craig discovered that rather than renovate a vintage machine, people tended to buy new retro-styles that don't breakdown. Yet it was his espresso machine, a much-treasured 1950s Faema, which stole the show, brewing coffee for scooter customers. And so his café started to grow.

Eventually Craig divided the business into ScooterCaffè and ScooterWorks. The scooters moved out of Lower Marsh and into new premises along the river near Tower Bridge. "I needed to break up the identity," he says. "We'd have people coming to the café asking for scooter parts and people going to the workshop looking for cocktails." The scooter business still keeps him busy. Some evenings he'll be on scooter recovery that involves driving round the city collecting broken-down scooters in his truck and taking them back to the workshop for repair.

The Faema has remained on the counter and continues to brew reliable coffees for its many followers. Beans are supplied by roasters Londinium Coffee and the blend changes regularly. By night, the café turns into a bar and on weekends you'll probably have to squeeze through the cluster of drinkers who huddle along the counter. The room is dotted with tiny tables just large enough for two and often you'll be lucky to find a vacant one. Much of the furniture and vintage treasures date from the 1950s and were finds from flea-markets and junk shops in Italy. It's very much a look that's evolved over the years. "It's an extension of my living room," says Craig, who lives upstairs.

In 2009 he cleared out all the spare scooter parts that had been collecting in the basement. He dug down another meter and converted the space into a second bar area, a dark, atmospheric den-like place. It's down here that ScooterCaffè holds film-nights. It's free and there's no need to book—you just turn up, buy a drink, and take a seat. On selected Saturday nights there's live music. Don't expect to find out about ScooterCaffè's events online, though, as Craig decided to do away with the cyber presence he'd once had. Keeping a low profile suits him much better. "Its really nice going old-school," he says. "We get a nice quality of people who choose to come here." The best way to find out what's going on at the café, it seems, is by becoming a regular.

Craig first came to London from New Zealand for a two-week trip in 1992. He went over to Italy for a few days where he met a guy who introduced him to some junk-yards. He started salvaging and was instantly hooked. He sold everything back home and with the cash in his back pocket he decided to set up a business in London. "If you have a great idea and want to work hard, London is easy," he says. "This is my fourth career. They've all been my hobbies. I started off as an aircraft technician, then a photographer in the Air Force and I trained as a pilot. And now this."

As for the menu, well, technically there isn't one. There are usually a couple of cakes on offer if you fancy a slice with your coffee but if you want more of a meal, you're invited to bring your own food in. "It was a practical consideration," says Craig. "Providing food can mean a hell of a lot of hassle." So they operate as a BYOF (Bring Your Own Food) and focus on providing quality drinks instead.

Craig retains his love for Italy and speaks the language fluently. "I've got an ear and taste for the language. I learnt it while travelling around," he says. He has a house in the hills near the north-eastern city of Trieste and escapes there every month. He still has various plans up his sleeve that he'd love to live out, from flying a plane for an aid company to riding his motorbike to China. He's grateful to be in the incredible position of doing something he loves. His philosophy? "Give back something and get more good luck," he says. "Sure, I could make more money but as long as I can pay my bills . . . I'm not going to chase someone down the street if they don't pay for their coffee." Chances are, though, you'll find it's worth every penny.

Tinto Coffee

411 Fulham Palace Road, Fulham SW6 6SX
020 7731 8232 www.tintocoffee.com
Open: 7AM–9PM Mon to Sun
Tube/rail: Putney Bridge, Parson's Green

TINTO COFFEE is the kind of place where you feel so at home you might be tempted to put your feet up as you sit down with your coffee. Walk past the counter and into the back room with its fireplace, wallpapered alcove and comfy seats and you'll feel like you've stepped into someone's living room. There's even a computer on a desk if you need to surf the net. "People feel so comfortable here," says Colombian co-owner Pablo Uribe. "We wanted it to feel neighbourhoody. Mismatched and eclectic, comfortable and cosy. It's not too thought out. That's the advantage you have as an independent."

From the moment Tinto's doors open at 7AM, the café starts to fill up. Weekdays bring a mix of workers and local residents, particularly mums who call in for their daily coffee after the school run. People who have their offices in the area drop by for lunch and weekends bring families who gather round tables for coffee and breakfast, spreading out with newspapers. And with Fulham's famous football ground, Craven Cottage, just down the road, the café fills up on match days with football fans marching down Fulham Palace Road on their way home.

It's easy to see why people who visit Tinto become regulars. "Customers have parcels

delivered here or they leave their keys with us," says Rob Baines, who owns the business with his partner Pablo. "It's not about making money—it's about having a facility for the whole neighbourhood. We used to open even later." The menu is simple and many items are given new twists and tweaks every week to keep it exciting. Everything's freshly made on site and the ingredients are locally sourced. "We make everything ourselves from brownies and carrot cake to pastries and croissants. It's an important part of the coffeehouse feel. It's a very hands-on thing," says Rob. There are gluten-free offerings including toast and brownies and cooked breakfast is served all day. "It's super popular," grins Rob. "The main thing for me when I have breakfast is that it's hot. Then I thought about the presentation. We serve ours in a cast iron pan and introduced a buzzer system so we can get it to the customer quickly when it's busy."

Tinto sits towards the Putney Bridge end of Fulham Palace Road on the stretch up to Hammersmith. The café overlooks Bishops Park that leads down to the River Thames and Fulham Palace, an estate once owned by London's bishops, with its botanic gardens, museum, garden centre and grand café. "Other cafés on this road don't last," says Rob. "People have said Tinto should not work because of its location but it's like an enigma—it does work." So what's the secret? "Good coffee and atmosphere," says Pablo.

Rob's interest in coffee began in his Canadian hometown of Vancouver during the late 1990s where he remembers being a regular at Starbucks' second store, after the success of their first in Seattle. He loved the coffeehouse concept and moved over to London where he set up Coffee Club Ltd, a café business located at Westminster Abbey and St Paul's Cathedral that targeted tourists. The company's office on Fulham Palace Road, near Rob's home, was larger than required, so in 1998 he and Pablo converted the front room into a coffee bar. They called it Tinto from the Colombian word meaning small black coffee. "London is so cosmopolitan, it embraces new concepts," says Rob. "It's the eye of the whole world. It's

an amazing place to open a business." Rob and Pablo have since founded Snog, the gourmet frozen yogurt chain with shops across London and overseas.

You'll find Paul Arbelaez, Tinto's manager and partner in the business, operating the coffee machine, shouting out the coffees as he lines them up along the side for customers to collect. Paul used to be a customer at Tinto before he started working there in 2002. Coffees are made with a darker roast and double shot as standard. "We serve it on the stronger side," says Rob. "Once you try stronger coffee a couple of times you can't go back."

During the spring and summer you can take your coffee into the adjoining garden that's part of a conservation area for local residents. Look for the gate on Colehill Gardens to the side of Tinto and its sign that reads "Tinto Garden, Open, Enjoy Nature." The trees, shrubs and flowers have been left to grow as nature intended. "The garden used to be like a bombsite, it was derelict. So we took it over and cleaned it all up," says Rob. Follow one of the dusty paths between the foliage to hidden benches and sit beneath the trees among the birdsong.

Rob and Pablo are both self-confessed perfectionists. Rob runs the business and takes care of the staff. Pablo focusses on the design and quality and Paul is a people person. "He knows everybody," says Pablo.

The Pavilion

Victoria Park, Corner Old Ford Road and Grove Park, Hackney, E9 7DE
020 8980 0030 www.the-pavilion-cafe.com
Open: 8AM-4.30PM Mon to Sun
Tube/rail: Bethnal Green, Cambridge Heath

"We're a breakfast cafe," says Rob Green, who owns The Pavilion with Brett Redman. "Breakfast can be a really special meal and we set out to do the best breakfast in London. But it goes much deeper than wanting just a great café—it's about building a community. We have a relaxed relationship with our customers and we're more like a community-service to the area." Set within East London's Victoria Park, The Pavilion is a fantastic venue with a lively community feel and great food. Hot breakfasts, from bacon sandwiches to pancakes with honeycomb butter and eggs Royale are whisked from the kitchen to tables of hungry customers. For lunch there are salads and savoury fritters and a rainbow selection of freshly squeezed juices to wash it down with.

On weekends it's easy to see why locals and visitors make a beeline for Victoria Park and gravitate towards The Pavilion. The park is credited as one of London's loveliest and is one of the oldest public parks in Britain. Located in the Borough of Tower Hamlets and spanning Hackney, Bow, and Bethnal Green, it's bordered by two canals. With its large lake and ponds, it makes a picturesque setting for outdoor festivals and concerts while retaining a laid-back vibe that you won't always find in other central London parks. Wander around its tree-lined paths and you'll see locals whiling away an afternoon with a book or feeding the ducks with their children. Gates dotted around its perimeter lead to quiet pockets of East London life and local hangouts, including boutiques, cafés and pubs around the small roundabout where Grove Road and Victoria Park Road intersect.

Those who venture into The Pavilion range from old to young, from dog-walkers and joggers to families and even fishermen. For many, the café is a cornerstone of their weekly routine. Order and pay at the counter and be prepared to share a table or hover for a seat at busy periods. Sip coffee al fresco under the trees overlooking the lake as children roll up on bikes and scooters and tuck into little tubs of ice cream. Rob and Brett, who both live locally, have managed to merge a whole cross-section of people in the community. "We're becoming proper Eastenders," smiles Rob.

Rob grew up in a foodie family (his granddad had always kept pigs and grew his own vegetables) and was a social worker for eight years. He then swapped the UK for Sri Lanka where he built up a tea business on a biodynamic tea-plantation and helped to build schools for children of tea-farming families. A year-and-a-half later, he returned to London and started selling his organic loose-leaf tea at Borough Market, one of London's largest and most popular foodie haunts. At the time, Brett, a professionally trained chef from Australia, was running a café called Elliot's in East London's Bethnal Green, where Rob was a regular customer. United by their love of food, the pair soon became friends. When the site in Victoria Park came up for tender in 2006, they started talking about setting up a café there together. After winning the bid, Brett closed down Elliot's and together they set about giving Victoria's Park's glass rotunda building a fresh redesign and opened with a new menu.

Instead of buying in produce from the big brands, Brett and Rob seek out small independent producers, artisans and growers from within their community. Their aim is to source everything from within a 30-mile radius of the café. They've even started growing some of their own produce on an allotment in a local primary school where they run a scheme to educate children about the provenance of food. "We're on a food voyage to be super-localised," says Rob. "It's small people doing small things and making a big impact." Smoked salmon comes from their "crazy Norwegian friend Olly" who smokes fish in his back garden up the road. Salad leaves come from another friend who runs a biodynamic farm and from family-run farm Chegworth Valley in Kent. Coffee beans from Bethnal Green's Square Mile roasters and sourdough bread from E5 Bakehouse in Hackney are so local that they are delivered by bicycle.

As well as tracking down the best local produce, Rob and Brett are on a mission to reduce packaging and waste. "It's just about communication," says Rob. "We love working with individuals—calling them up, visiting them." The un-homogenized milk they use comes from a farm in Kent. It's supplied in 13-liter bag-in-boxes and does away with plastic cartons that would otherwise pile up in the bin. They plan to make the milk accessible to other London cafés via a co-operative scheme. "It's good fresh milk from a single herd of seventy cows. The idea is that other cafés can piggy-back on our adventures," says Rob.

Brett and Rob invest as much in their staff as their produce. "All our staff live locally and there's a big cross-section of nationalities. No one's left since we opened," says Rob. Some staff are recruited from Jamie Oliver's apprentice chef scheme Fifteen, which offers training for young people from deprived backgrounds. "We want to create a fertile environment for kids to work in and Jamie was a big influence on all of us," says Rob.

In addition to operating as a daytime café, The Pavilion has also hosted pop-up suppers against the backdrop of the lake. Elliot's in Bethnal Green may have closed its doors but, in July 2011, Rob and Brett opened a brand new Elliot's, a café-restaurant in Borough Market near

London Bridge. Brett runs the kitchen and the menu showcases the best of the market's produce. It's about small plates, great coffee, and a relaxed atmosphere. With The Pavilion and Elliot's to run between them, Brett and Rob strive to continue being a resource to everyone connected to the two cafés. "We'll keep driving on," says Rob. "With two sites we can give people better opportunities and new motivation."

Bar Italia

22 Frith Street, Soho W1D 4RF
020 7437 4520 www.baritaliasoho.co.uk
Open: 6AM–5AM Mon to Fri, 6AM–3AM Sun
Tube/rail: Leicester Square,
Tottenham Court Road

IT IS IMPOSSIBLE TO TALK about Bar Italia without touching upon the history of Soho over the past few decades. In 1949 Italian immigrants Lou and Caterina Polledri saw a niche for a proper Italian coffee bar in London. They opened Bar Italia in Soho, the heart of what was London's thriving Italian community. Bar Italia operated as much as an Italian social centre as a coffee bar. It was a place where artisans from knife-grinders and stonecutters to the ice men who delivered to the restaurants would gather to catch up on news from back home or to find work. If you wanted to find out who was well or unwell, who'd died and who'd been born, you'd go to Bar Italia.

In the 1970s, Lou and Caterina's son Nino took over Bar Italia. By this time Soho had become infamous for its seedy bars and you couldn't move for sex shops. Soho's ties with the sex industry were nothing new. Since the eighteenth century, the area within the four roads that marked the boundary of Soho (Oxford Street, Regent Street, Charing Cross Road and Shaftesbury Avenue) had entertained a colourful mix of brothels, strip-clubs, and riotous bars. But it was during the 1970s that the sex shops started to multiply to such an extent that Westminster Council was forced to step in to close illegal premises. As a result, the sex industry in Soho dwindled.

In the 1980s, it was the music industry that gripped the area. Bar Italia witnessed the comings and goings of pop-stars and musicians, many of whom used the café as their second office. The 1980s also marked the beginning of the café revolution. Bar Italia was the first establishment to open until 5am and with the cleaner opening up at 6am, they were virtually a 24-hour operation.

Today Nino's children Antonio, Luigi, and Veronica run the business. Antonio remembers being taken to Bar Italia every weekend as a child. He recalls the Maltese standing in doorways in their string vests and people looking for a hustle. "It was like a scene out of Goodfellas," he says. "Soho has always had a very vivid, high-profile street life."

Bar Italia claims to be London's most famous coffee bar. There is even a musical about it, written by former Eurythmics member Dave Stewart. The café is still a favourite haunt of celebrities who can hide away at the back knowing they won't be interrupted. A huge photograph of Rocky Marciano, the Italian-American world heavyweight champion of the 1950s, dominates the wall. Caterina Polledri had famously cooked for him the peasant-style Italian food—polenta and risotto—that he was craving and unable to find in Soho. The picture was a gift to the Polledri family from Rocky's widow. Other photographs capture Frith Street throughout the decades and are a fascinating portrayal of the area.

The interior remains largely untouched. The original stone floor, laid by Antonio's Great Uncle Torino, bears testament to the millions of people who have walked across it over the years. The red and white Formica on the walls remains and customers can still perch on high stools along the long narrow bar opposite the counter. Italian cakes in pretty boxes, bunches of garlic, and an oversized Italian flag hang from the ceiling and Italian football shirts are pinned up at the windows. *Calico*—Italian football—continues to be an important part of Bar Italia and matches are still screened here, as they have been for years, though today the screen is larger and flatter.

Next-door to Bar Italia is Little Italy, a restaurant also owned by the Polledri family. And three doors down the other way, numbers 23a and 23b Frith Street still bear the name A. Angelucci

Coffee Specialists, a family-run business that started roasting coffee in Soho in 1929. Angelucci has since relocated to north London and their former Frith Street shop has now been incorporated into a sandwich bar called Nino's Paninos, which is also owned by the Polledris. The original Gaggia espresso machine at Bar Italia has been brewing Angelucci's secret blend of beans into Italian-style coffees for over 50 years. "No gimmicks, no syrups, no nonsense," says Antonio. All the coffees are tailor-made and regulars, many of whom are Italian, don't even need to ask for their coffee. On the menu you'll find paninis and salads. Pizzas are made on site and cooked in the oven in the basement and many of the Italian cakes are made next door at Little Italy.

Since the 1990s, the "big boys"—the corporate coffeehouse chains—moved into Soho, popping up almost on every corner. Family-owned Italian businesses have gradually diminished to little more than a handful. "It has its ups and downs," says Antonio. "We are the last bit of the Italian section left."

Yet Bar Italia is still going strong in the heart of so much that London is famous for—its theatres, restaurants, bars, and clubs. Across the road is legendary Ronnie Scott's, one of the oldest jazz clubs in the world. Sit at one of the tables on the pavement outside Bar Italia early in the morning as Soho is waking up and you'll see chefs smoking in doorways and couples drinking coffee in the sun. Go at night and soak up a slice of Soho at its liveliest.

The Providores and Tapa Room

109 Marylebone High Street, W1U 4RX
020 7935 6175 www.theprovidores.co.uk
Open: 9AM-10.30PM Mon to Fri, 10AM-10.30PM Sat, 10AM-10PM Sun (Tapa Room)
Tube: Baker Street, Bond Street, Regent's Park

WHEN PETER GORDON and Michael McGrath opened The Providores and Tapa Room in 2001 with two friends they set out to create a New Zealand-style café that was women-friendly. Their vision for the Tapa Room was a wine-bar and café that was warm and cosy and stayed open into the evening. "We wanted the casual all-day thing," says Peter, a New Zealander, who is executive chef of the operation. "We really were the vanguard of that in London. Somewhere you could come in at 8 o'clock at night for a coffee and no one's going to give you the evil eye." They called the ground-floor the Tapa Room because of the large, decorative tapa cloth—a gift from the mother of one of their friends—that's displayed on the wall opposite the bar. Originating from the Pacific Islands, tapa cloths are made from hand-painted paper bark and are traditionally used as clothing and decorative pieces in the home and at ceremonies.

Marylebone High Street and its surrounding streets are known for their residents including writers, musicians, statesmen, doctors, and artists from years gone by to the present day. Much of Marylebone Village, including over 300 English Heritage Listed buildings, is owned by the Howard de Walden Estate. "It's their vision of the street that keeps it unique," says Peter. Today people flock here for stylish shops and bars and restaurants. "We have a lot of residents around here," says Peter. "Schools are here, women are out shopping..."

You'll find The Providores and Tapa Room in an attractive red brick building with arched windows. Upstairs is given over to the more formal dining room, The Providores. In the Tapa Room the New Zealand theme is subtle but take a closer look and you'll see the clock that's set to Kiwi time and much of the art and quirky artefacts—including the upside-down plants hanging at the window—are by Kiwi artists. And for lovers of Kiwi wine, the Tapa Room offers the largest range of New Zealand wine in the UK.

The Tapa Room immediately struck a chord with Marylebone locals and those from further afield who appreciated the good coffee, lovely food and the table service. There are no bookings and from day one customers have happily queued into the street for a seat. On weekends the queues never stop. Some locals go three times a day. The kitchen turns out around 600 brunches every weekend and on Sundays poaches at least 400 eggs. Solo diners may be asked to slot into one of the seats in the window among the stacks of food magazines to browse through.

The high ceiling gives the room a sense of space and the raised communal table seats rows of diners who delve into plates of food, talking ten to the dozen. Staff flit between tables and hover over shoulders taking orders and setting down wonderful looking plates of food and coffees that keep on coming. There are trays of freshly made tarts and muffins on the bar and bowls of fresh fruit. The whole place is buzzing and convivial.

"The brekkie menu is typical Kiwi brunch—fry-ups, Turkish eggs. Lots of dishes are made to share and we keep adding things on to the menu and not taking others off. Anything's game in our kitchen," smiles Peter. "There are certain things we won't put on out of season. Wild garlic and new spuds—we find that exciting." All ingredients are sourced with care. Their eggs and milk are organic, fish is sustainably caught and meat comes from farms where animal welfare standards are high. Grains, pulses, and nuts come from an organic hippie company. "We love buying from suppliers who we know little stories about," Peter says.

Coffee is by established roasters Monmouth, who have been roasting and retailing in London since 1978. "It's really good, well-traded coffee with consistent roasts," says Peter. "People now take coffee seriously. When I first arrived in London in 1989 you'd get instant coffee. Now people aren't necessarily after the large litre coffee. They're prepared to pay a bit extra for quality over quantity. It's changed so dramatically. There is definitely an increasing appreciation of barista-made coffee in London, very similar to New Zealand."

TRADITIONAL LONDON CAFFS

WITH ITS FRILLY CURTAINS IN THE WINDOWS, fixed seating, and tiled walls, the traditional 1950s London caff became famous for dishing up large servings of ambience as much as its all-day breakfast.

Often run by family members, these cafés offer a hearty welcome and home-cooked food that's kind to the wallet and generous to the waistline. Peg-board menus promise old family recipes and fixed daily specials whose origins have become local legends. In some, the espresso machine is rivalled by a stainless steel countertop boiler, essential for brewing gallons of sweet, milky tea. In others, coffee is simply poured from a jug.

And then there's the vintage décor—leatherette banquettes and easy-wipe Formica tables were once the height of luxury. Shelves behind the counter display postcards and photographs of grandchildren and the celebrities who once ate there and were snapped posing with the owners.

Customers from all walks of life slip into their favourite seats, make do without WiFi, and always pay by cash. For many, the caff is a home away from home—their kitchen, living room, and dining room rolled into one. Start going regularly and you'll soon start to pick out familiar faces who appear at set times each day.

Since fast food and coffeehouse chains moved into the high streets in the 1990s, rising rents have forced many independent café owners out. Let's hope the traditional caffs that remain are here to stay. They deserve to be cherished.

E. Pellicci

332 Bethnal Green Road, Bethnal Green E2 0AG
020 7739 4873
Open: 7AM-4PM Mon to Sat
Tube/rail: Bethnal Green, Cambridge Heath

NEVIO PELLICCI, E. Pellicci's late owner, was famous for his ties. He'd wear one every day. Customers would bring him ties back as presents whenever they went on holiday. A creature of habit, he'd never miss Mass on a Sunday. "After, he'd walk to Columbia Road to get his winkles and prawns and go for a drink in the pub," recalls his daughter Anna. "Then we'd all sit down for Sunday lunch at 2.30, 3 o'clock." Nevio was born in the room above his parents' Bethnal Green café in 1925. On the day of his funeral, 82 years later, crowds turned out to pay their respects. Police closed the road and escorted the traditional Cockney horse-drawn procession.

Today Signor Pellicci watches over his former home and café from a photograph behind the

counter. His wife Maria has continued to run the business with her children Anna and Nevio (Little Nev). Her other daughter Bruna helps out sometimes on Saturdays and Anna and Nev's cousin Toni has worked at the café since 1970. The Pellicci children grew-up in a terraced house around the corner and café customers became an extension of the family. "The café seems like home," Anna says. "We'd be here before school and straight after school. There would be a big dinner here every night with all the family in the room at the back."

E. Pellicci was Elide, Nevio Senior's mother, who came over from Italy and set up the café in 1900 with her husband Priamo. You can see the couple in black-and-white photographs on the wall in the café. They lived in the two rooms upstairs and Nevio was the youngest of their seven children. "The girls slept here and the boys here," says Anna, pointing to two spots on the ceiling above customers' heads. The bathroom was a tin bath in the backyard and family meals were cooked downstairs in the café. Elide's husband Priamo died soon after Nevio was born and Elide brought up the children and ran the café herself. Little Nev remembers his grandmother as being quite a woman. "She couldn't speak English but she could swear well apparently," he smiles.

Now in its third-generation, the family-run business offers intimacy and warmth that café chains so often lack. Service is swift and friendly, the food is keenly priced and portions are generous. Music is provided by the radio behind the counter and there's lots of lively banter across the tables. At busy periods you'll be expected to squeeze in to share your table.

Peer through the serving hatch into the kitchen at the back of the café and you'll see Anna and Little Nev's mother Maria at the stove. Now in her 70s, Maria still lives around the corner and works at the café as she has always done. Periodically during the day she'll pop home. "To do

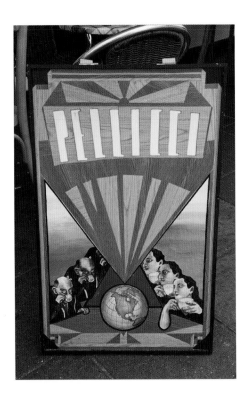

more work, like putting the washing on," says Nev. All the food is made by Maria. Pies are served straight from the oven and depending which day you go, there might be chicken and mushroom pie with peas and carrots or steak and kidney pie with broccoli cheese. There are lasagnes, speciality pastas, and on Fridays fish and chips. Maria cuts the chips by hand and makes the pastries for the pies. Food sometimes spills over the sides of the white plates and there are squeezy bottles of sauce on the tables. For dessert there's Maria's apple pie, bread pudding and lemon polenta cake.

The stainless steel boiler on the counter, with one outlet for hot water and one for steam, has been there longer than anyone can remember. It harkens back to an era when customers used to order sweet, milky tea and is now so old that it's almost impossible to find someone who can service it. Today the café serves more coffee than tea and the boiler vies for space on the counter with an espresso machine.

In the 1940s, Elide had the café walls panelled with the distinctive Art Deco-style wooden marquetry, believed to be walnut and maple. The work of Italian carpenter Achille Capocci, he started with the simple engraving of the initials EP in the woodwork behind the counter. "Elide Pellicci, not Elvis Presley!" laughs Anna. He completed one panel at a time, as Elide saved up to pay him, and the interior now has English Heritage Grade II listing.

Jimmy Phimister—an old rock 'n' roll collector known as Jukebox Jimmy—has been coming to E. Pellicci since before Anna and Nev were born. Originally from Fife in Scotland, he moved down to the East End with his family as a boy. "I'm a Jockney," he grins. He grew up round the back of the café, although has since moved to Poplar, a couple of miles to the east. He remembers the notorious Kray twins, Reggie and Ronnie, the East End gangsters of the 1950s and '60s, and used to play Penny Up the Wall as a child with their nephew Gary. At Ronnie's funeral in 2005, he recalls talking to an American news reporter and seeing Reggie—on special release from prison to attend the funeral—handcuffed to a guard.

Jukebox Jimmy takes the bus from Poplar to E. Pellicci six days a week for his lunch. "It's around 11 o' clock, so I call it brunch. Curry or roast dinner. Every summer, when the café closes for a month, I lose a stone," he says. "You get every type of person here. I once sat and talked to Jools Holland (the musician and television presenter) over the table at the back. Here you must talk. You're thrown together." E. Pellicci has seen its share of celebrities over the years as the autograph book that Toni keeps behind the counter will confirm. It's packed with messages and photographs of soap-stars, actors, and singers.

Bethnal Green has a large Bangladeshi community and the lively street market that runs up Bethnal Green Road is still going strong. In recent years artists have moved into the area and property prices have shot up. "Years ago you'd get real regulars. Workers from the breweries and docks," says Nev. "Now it's anyone and everyone." Chatting to customers, whoever they may be, is second nature to the Pelliccis. "I love the atmosphere and meeting people," says Anna. "It sounds corny but when people go out happy, it's nice." If only the panelled walls could talk. You can only imagine the characters they've met and the stories they've amassed over the years.

Regency Café

17-19 Regency Street, Pimlico, SW1P 4BY
020 7821 6596
Open: 7AM-2.30PM and 4PM-7.15PM Mon to Fri, 7AM-midday Sat
Tube/rail: St James's Park, Pimlico, Victoria

CUSTOMERS GO TO Regency Café as much for its striking décor as for the home-cooked food. Set in a glorious 1950s time warp, the vintage interior of this proper old-style English caff would be almost impossible to replicate. Brown plastic chairs and Formica tables are fixed to the floor and red-and-white checked curtains are pulled across the lower half of the windows. Natural light is boosted by simple flourescent strips overhead and walls are tiled floor-to-ceiling.

Thanks to its preserved décor, the café is hired out for advertising and magazine location shoots and has been used as a film-set for feature films including Layer Cake and Brighton Rock. "For Brighton Rock, they completely re-did it as the 1960s," says Claudia Perotti, who runs the café with Marco Schiavetta. "They stuck sea paraphernalia all over the walls and changed the curtains in the windows. We had a row of Vespas outside and people in cool '60s outfits."

You'll find either Claudia or Marco manning the cash-register behind the counter. From their spot here they'll take over 200 orders a day, relaying them to the kitchen and ensuring that plates of food go out to the right customers. "We basically run the whole shebang," says Claudia. "You have to be a multi-tasker. Sometimes it's crazy and we're run off our feet. The speed comes with experience and we've got faster and faster. Get stressed and the customers get stressed too." It's a seemingly never-ending cycle of meal management from dawn till dusk and from the moment you step through the door you'll be swept along with the flow. At busy times you'll inch steadily along the counter towards Claudia at the helm of the military-like operation. Softly spoken,

she'll confirm your order and take your money. And then, in a voice that comes from deep within her slight frame, she'll belt out the names of dishes as they land next to her from the kitchen, her voice resounding over the din of 60-plus diners. Customers, complying with the drill, return to the counter to collect their meals, then grab cutlery from a metal tin and duck back to their seats to tuck in. "You've got to have a big voice. You've got to be heard," Claudia says.

The two menus at Regency Café are Breakfast and Lunch/Evening. It's standard home-cooked British fare with fixed weekly specials as follows: braised steak on Monday, shepherd's pie on Tuesday, curry on Wednesday, roast pork on Thursday and fish and chips on Friday. "The menu's more of a suggestion than fixed," says Claudia. Breakfasts are Full English (and variations of) and all main dishes are served with chips and salad or vegetables, with bottles of condiments on the tables to squeeze over. Desserts are traditional sponges and pies that are served hot in bowls with custard or cream. For smaller appetites there are filled rolls and sandwiches, and cold drinks and chocolate bars from the chiller-cabinet. The café's three chefs—one for prep and two short-order cooks—work their way through six 25-kilo bags of potatoes a day for chips alone which they cut by hand, nice and thick.

Customers are a true mix and at least 95 percent are regulars. Gas-men and plumbers pop in first thing for steaming mugs of tea and for sandwiches to takeout or a sit-down cooked breakfast. People pour in through-out the day from nearby offices and organizations in-cluding Channel 4 Television, the Tate Britain gallery, and the Home Office. The evening brings families with young children, taxi-drivers and shift-workers who call in for an early evening meal. Other locals drop by for a hot meal to line their stomachs before heading off to the pub.

Catering is in Claudia's blood. "It's all I've ever known," she says. London born and bred, she grew

up working in her family's restaurant on Villiers Street, near Embankment. In 1986, her family sold the business and took over Regency Café, a mile away near Pimlico, with their friends, the Schiavetta family. The café, instantly recognizable with its name spelt out in bold white lettering against the striking black façade, had been run by mutual friends of the two families since the 1950s. Originally believed to be a pub because of the trap-door on the pavement that gives access to the cellar, the premises was then home to a pawn-shop before its incarnation as a café.

Claudia is a whirlwind of efficiency and speed and it's easy to see how the café takes up all of her energy. "You have to have your wits about you," she says. "It sounds a bit crazy but the customers help you along. You want to do well for them.

River Café

1a Station Approach, Putney Bridge SW6 3UH
020 7736 6296
Open: 6.30AM-3.30PM Mon to Sat
Tube/rail: Putney Bridge

NOT TO BE CONFUSED WITH West London's Michelin-starred restaurant of the same name, River Café at Putney Bridge is tucked into a quiet row of shops—a newsagents, a hairdressers and a greengrocers—and its preserved sign on the front promises Fresh Cut Sandwiches and Light Refreshments. The site on Station Approach started life in the 1880s as a dairy though it has been a café since the mid-1950s. It's been in the Vernazza family since 1978 and is owned by Lorenzo and Renata who moved to the UK from northern Italy in the

1960s. They run the café with their daughter Liliana, their son Robert and his wife Alex. Sit down inside with a mug of tea and a plate of hot food and you'll be transported back to an era that knew neither WiFi nor mobile phones.

Staff behind the counter expertly go about their business, speedily buttering bread, stacking crockery and pouring coffee from a jug. Customers trickle in to queue at the counter while others settle into seats, stir sugar into their tea, and spread a newspaper onto the table to read as they eat. Sometimes the quiet chatting is punctuated by a laugh or an excited voice. The telephone behind the counter rings intermittently and chairs scrape across the floor as people come and go. "We treat our customers as we'd like to be treated ourselves," says Robert. "It's a relaxed atmosphere."

Lorenzo does the cooking with two other chefs—one has been at River Café for over 20 years. For Lorenzo and Robert, the day begins soon after 5am when they arrive at the café. "We switch on all the machines and get everything ready," says Robert. "Then the chefs arrive and get all the prep done—they'll bake the jam tarts, rock cakes, and apple pie and roast any joints of meat that need cooking." As breakfast gets underway and Putney Bridge stirs to life, bus drivers pop in for teas and coffees. At regular intervals throughout the morning Lorenzo will appear from the kitchen through a squeaky door that doubles as a serving hatch. With a pepper mill tucked into the ties of his white apron, he'll carry plates of food to waiting customers, clearing tables on his way back to the kitchen. The cooked breakfast at River Cafe—a mix and match selection of eggs, bacon, sausage, beans and more—is something of a speciality. "It's English breakfast made by Italians," smiles Robert. There's no need to limit yourself to breakfast, though. Hot meals are served as soon as doors open at 6.30am and include pasta dishes, omelettes and British classics such as shepherd's pie, mixed grill, and liver and bacon. For more modest appetites there are filled baguettes and sandwiches that are toasted then wrapped in paper bags for takeout.

As well as bus drivers, customers are local residents, builders, and workers from nearby offices. Tourists from the hotel round the corner call in for breakfast. Work-men in overalls swig the last of their tea, wipe their faces with paper napkins, and hand their empty plates back to Lorenzo. On selected Sundays, the café caters for the football crowd visiting Fulham's ground nearby.

You'll find a simple room with coffee-coloured woodwork and a well-trod lino floor. There's an old clock on the wood-panelled back wall, flourescent tubes above and old blinds rolled up at the windows. There's a staircase that leads to the first floor but this is for staff only. The original blue and cream tiles on the walls remain from the site's days as a former dairy. Set into the shiny tiles are mirrors and poster-sized holiday prints of Venetian and Sicilian landscapes— now faded over the years—taken in the late 1960s by

Lorenzo. Behind the counter, shelves display family photographs and, pasted to the wall, you'll see posters of the Italian football team posing after their World Cup victory of 1982.

Opposite the café is Putney Bridge Underground Station though at its westerly point here the tracks run above ground. The road serves as a turning point for the buses that hover in the stands outside, their engines ticking over as drivers wait for passengers to arrive from trains. Bus drivers pace around, smoking and drinking tea. Despite its south west postcode, Putney Bridge is on the north side of the Thames. Around the corner is the New King's Road, winding its way towards Chelsea, and Fulham High Street that runs over the bridge into Putney on the south side of the river.

A passageway alongside the railway leads to a riverside walk or you can climb the steps and follow the tracks across the river on a footbridge that trembles when a train clatters past. Look across the river to a row of trees marking the edge of Wandsworth Park and to Thames-side mansions with grassy gardens that lead down to the water's edge. Walking up to the bridge and taking in this peaceful view is the perfect excuse to walk off a plate of home-cooked food at River Café.

The Shepherdess

221 City Rd, EC1V 1JN
020 7253 2463
Open: 6.30AM-4PM Mon to Fri, 7AM-3PM Sat
Tube/rail: Old Street

WHAT'S NOT TO LOVE about the Shepherdess café? It's always buzzing, the servings are huge, and the staff know the value of a smile. Come here for a proper cooked breakfast or lunch and you won't leave hungry. On the laminated menu you'll find a page-long list of sandwiches from peanut butter to salt beef and hot dishes from jacket potatoes with various toppings to chops, scampi, and steaks. Dishes are homemade and most come with chips or salad. Desserts are apple or cherry pies, doughnuts, buns, and scones, all served with ice cream, cream, or custard.

The Sherpherdess is owned by Nick Menegatos. Originally from the Greek island of Kefalonia, Nick came to London with his wife Vicky. He'd travelled the world as a Second Officer in the Navy, then worked as a taxi driver in Athens. After the city's earthquake in 1981 the couple decided to move to London. It was Nick's brother-in-law who gave him the idea of running a café. Nick had never done anything like it before yet he was up for the challenge. "Nothing is difficult, all except here," Nick says, tapping his head.

And so he took over The Shepherdess. The previous owner agreed to show him the ropes, then didn't turn up after the first week, leaving Nick to run the show. He didn't speak much English and his cooking skills were minimal. He'd never even cooked an egg before running the café. "I lost

five kilos in the first week," he says. He quickly learned how to fry an egg and became an expert at making apple pie. He knew he could achieve anything he put his mind to. "I had a lot of power, here," he says, tapping his head again.

Nick spent weekends fixing anything in the café that needed attention, saving money by doing it himself. He was the café's plumber, electrician and decorator. "I tried my best," he says. "If something breaks, open it up and have a look. Ninety percent of the time it fixes." There were no deliveries back then and it was a hard slog. For years he'd open up at 5 o'clock every morning and end the day at the cash and carry, unloading shopping outside the café at 10 o'clock at night in the dark. Every Monday he'd be down at Smithfield meat market a mile away. Yet his customers kept him going. "The English people are nice, polite and clever. I never had a complaint from an English person," he says. Back then he remembers having to explain to them what a cappuccino was.

The site has been a café for over 80 years. You'll still find the original cosy booths around the window and the signage outside has been there for as long as Nick can remember. It was Nick, though, who painted the curtains on the windows that have become one of the café's most distinguishing features. Framed photographs on the wall depict aqua seas, quiet coves and beach-side villas of Kefalonia.

The café is on the fringe of fashionable Hoxton with its bars, restaurants and art scene including Hoxton Square's world-famous art gallery, White Cube. City Road leads up to King's Cross, known for its international station St Pancras with direct links to Paris. In recent years many of the old warehouses in the streets around Shepherdess Walk have been converted into studios and loft-style apartments with impressive price-tags.

When Nick arrived in 1982, the area was dead. "There were two foreigners—me and the guy from South Africa who had the sweet shop over the road," he says. Today there's a mix of nationalities and Nick believes it's only a matter of time before the financial City of London creeps up through the area and towards King's Cross. Now in his 60s with two grown-up children, Nick has managed to ease back on the hours he puts in at the café. "Now I'm a little bit tired here, mentally," he says, tapping his head again. His egg-frying days might be over but you'll still find him at The Shepherdess where you'll be guaranteed a warm welcome and a memorable plate of food.

ACKNOWLEDGMENTS

To research this book I consumed beyond my lifetime's allowance of caffeine and ate at least twice my body weight in sandwiches and brownies, whilst feebly convincing myself I'd be walking them off. Sometimes, three coffees down, I'd imagine myself in one of London's old coffeehouses, buzzing with words and inspiration. On rainy days, holed up in a steamy caff with a plate of chips and a mug of tea, dragging myself out of the cozy banquette was as much as I could muster.

A huge thank you to: Michel and everyone at Interlink for commissioning the book and for all your advice; Hannah and Harry for the beautiful photographs that capture so much; James McDonald for design; Ramon Elinevsky for editing; Pam Fontes-May for production; Gayatri Kumar for proofreading; Mintel for providing data in the main introduction; Leon for your tireless encouragement and for reading every word; Joey and Essie for your eagle eyes; mum and dad for all the coffees and sandwiches over the years; and to the team at Browns for the countless coffees and chocolate muffins which have been the fuel of many words. Finally to all the café owners for sharing their incredible stories, as without you there would be no *Café Life London*.

CAFE LISTINGS

Bar Italia
22 Frith Street, Soho W1D 4RF
020 7437 4520 www.baritaliasoho.co.uk
Open: 6AM-5AM Mon to Fri, 6AM-3AM Sun
Tube/rail: Leicester Square,
Tottenham Court Road

Browns of Brockley
5 Coulgate Street, Brockley SE4 2RW
020 8692 0722
Open: 7.30AM-6PM Mon-Fri, 9AM-5PM Sat,
10AM-4PM Sun Rail: Brockley

Brunswick House Café
Brunswick House,
30 Wandsworth Road, Vauxhall SW8 2LG
020 7720 2926 www.brunswickhousecafe.co.uk
Open: 8AM-5PM Mon, 8AM-11.30PM Tues to Fri,
10AM-11.30PM Sat, 10AM-5PM Sun
Tube/rail: Vauxhall

Climpson & Sons
67 Broadway Market, Hackney E8 4PH
020 7812 9829 www.webcoffeeshop.co.uk
Open: 8AM-5PM Mon to Fri, 8.30AM-5PM Sat,
9AM-4PM Sun
Rail: Cambridge Heath, London Fields,
Haggerston

The Counter Café
7 Roach Road, Fish Island E3 2PA
07834 275 920 www.thecountercafe.co.uk
Open: 7.30AM-5PM Mon to Weds, 7.30AM-late Thurs to Fri,
8.30AM-late Sat, 8.30AM-5PM Sun
Tube/rail/DLR: Hackney Wick,
Pudding Mill DLR

The Deptford Project Café
121-123 Deptford High Street,
Deptford SE8 4NS
07545 593279 www.thedeptfordproject.com
Open 10AM-5.30PM Mon, Tues, Thurs, 9AM-5.30PM Weds,
Fri, Sat, 10AM-4.30PM Sun
Rail/DLR: Deptford, Deptford Bridge

Dose
70 Long Lane, EC1A 9EJ
020 7600 0382 www.dose-espresso.com
Open: 7AM-5PM Mon to Fri, 9AM-4PM Sat
Tube/rail: Barbican, Farringdon, St Paul's, City Thameslink

E. Pellicci
332 Bethnal Green Road,
Bethnal Green E2 0AG
020 7739 4873
Open: 7AM-4PM Mon to Sat
Tube/rail: Bethnal Green,
Cambridge Heath

Fernandez & Wells
73 Beak Street, Soho W1F 9SR
020 7287 8124 www.fernandezandwells.com
Open: 7.30AM-6PM Mon to Fri,
9AM-6PM Sat, 9AM-5PM Sun
Tube: Piccadilly Circus, Oxford Circus,
Tottenham Court Road

Flat White
17 Berwick Street, Soho W1F 0PT
020 7734 0370 www.flatwhitecafe.com
Open: 8AM-7PM Mon to Fri, 9AM-6PM Sat and Sun
Tube/rail: Oxford Circus,
Piccadilly Circus, Tottenham Court Road

La Fleur
  18 Royal Hill, Greenwich SE10 8RT
  020 8305 1772 www.la-fleur.co.uk
  Open: 7AM-4.30PM Mon-Sat, 11AM-3PM Sun
  Rail/DLR: Greenwich, Cutty Sark

Kaffeine
  66 Great Titchfield Street,
  Fitzrovia W1W 7GJ
  020 7580 6755 www.kaffeine.co.uk
  Open: 7.30AM-6PM Mon to Fri,
  9AM-6PM Sat, 9.30AM-5PM Sun
  Tube: Oxford Circus, Great Portland Street,
  Goodge Street, Tottenham Court Road

Lantana
  13 Charlotte Place, Fitzrovia W1T 1SN
  020 7637 3347 www.lantanacafe.co.uk
  Open (Lantana IN): 9AM-6PM Mon to Fri,
  9AM-5PM Sat and Sun
  Tube: Goodge Street,
  Tottenham Court Road

Look Mum No Hands!
  49 Old Street, EC1V 9HX
  020 7253 1025 www.lookmumnohands.com
  Open: 7.30AM-10PM Mon to Fri, 9AM-10PM Sat,
  10AM-10PM Sun
  Tube/rail: Old Street

Minkie's Deli
  Glasshouse, Chamberlayne Road,
  Kensal Rise NW10 5RQ
  020 8969 2182 www.minkiesdeli.co.uk
  Open: 7.30AM-7PM Mon to Sat, 8AM-4PM Sun
  Tube/Rail: Kensal Rise, Kensal Green

Munson's Coffee & Eats Co.
  73 St Mary's Road, Ealing W5 5RG
  020 8840 4114 www.munsons.co.uk
  Open: 7AM-6PM Mon to Fri,
  8AM-6PM Sat and Sun
  Tube/rail: South Ealing, Ealing Broadway

Notes Music & Coffee
  31 St Martin's Lane, WC2N 4ER
  020 7240 0424 www.notesmusiccoffee.com
  Open: 7.30AM-9PM, Thurs-Fri 7.30AM-10PM,
  Sat 9AM-10PM, Sun 10AM-6PM
  Tube/rail: Charing Cross,
  Leicester Square, Covent Garden

Orange Pekoe
  3 White Hart Lane, Barnes SW13 0PX
  020 8876 6070 www.orangepekoeteas.com
  Open: 7.30AM-5.30PM Mon to Fri,
  9AM-5.30PM Sat to Sun
  Rail: Barnes Bridge

The Pavilion
  Victoria Park, Corner Old Ford Road and Grove Park,
  Hackney, E9 7DE
  020 8980 0030 www.the-pavilion-cafe.com
  Open: 8AM-4.30PM Mon to Sun
  Tube/rail: Bethnal Green, Cambridge Heath

Petitou
  63 Choumert Road, Peckham SE15 4AR
  020 7639 2613 www.petitou.co.uk
  Open: 9AM-5.30PM Mon to Sat,
  10AM-5.30PM Sun
  Rail: Peckham Rye

The Providores and Tapa Room
  109 Marylebone High Street, W1U 4RX
  020 7935 6175 www.theprovidores.co.uk
  Open: 9AM-10.30PM Mon to Fri, 10AM-10.30PM Sat,
  10AM-10PM Sun (Tapa Room)
  Tube: Baker Street, Bond Street,
  Regent's Park

Prufrock Coffee
  23-25 Leather Lane, Clerkenwell EC1N 7TE
  020 7404 3597 www.prufrockcoffee.com
  Open: 8AM-6PM Mon to Fri, 10AM-4.30PM Sat, 11-4PM Sun
  Tube/rail: Chancery Lane, Farringdon

Queen's Wood Café
  Queen's Lodge, 42 Muswell Hill Road,
  Highgate N10 3JP
  020 8444 2604 www.queenswoodcafe.co.uk
  Open: 10AM-5PM Mon to Sun
  Tube: Highgate

Regency Café
  17-19 Regency Street, Pimlico, SW1P 4BY
  020 7821 6596
  Open: 7AM-2.30PM and 4PM-7.15PM
  Mon to Fri, 7AM-midday Sat
  Tube/rail: St James's Park, Pimlico, Victoria

River Café
  1a Station Approach,
  Putney Bridge SW6 3UH
  Tel: 020 7736 6296
  Open: 6.30AM-3.30PM Mon to Sat
  Tube/rail: Putney Bridge

Royal Teas
  76 Royal Hill, Greenwich, SE10 8RT
  020 8691 7240 www.royalteascafe.co.uk
  Open: 9.30AM-5.30PM Mon to Fri,
  10AM-6PM Sat, 10AM-5.30PM Sun
  Rail/DLR: Greenwich, Cutty Sark

Sacred
  13 Ganton Street, Soho W1F 9BL
  020 7734 1415 www.sacredcafe.co.uk
  Open: 7.30AM-8PM Mon to Fri,
  10AM-7PM Sat and Sun
  Tube: Oxford Circus, Piccadilly Circus

ScooterCaffè
  132 Lower Marsh, Waterloo SE1 7AE
  020 7620 1421
  Open: 8.30AM-11PM Mon to Thurs,
  8.30AM-midnight Fri to Sat, noon-10PM Sun
  Tube/rail: Lambeth North, Waterloo,
  Waterloo East

The Shepherdess
  221 City Rd, EC1V 1JN
  020 7253 2463
  Open: 6.30AM-4PM Mon to Fri, 7AM-3PM Sat
  Tube/rail: Old Street

Taylor Street Baristas
  22 Brook Mews, Mayfair W1K 4DY
  020 7629 3163 www.taylor-st.com
  Open: 7.30AM-5PM Mon to Fri
  Tube: Bond Street

The Tea Rooms
  153-155 Stoke Newington Church Street,
  Stoke Newington N16 0UH
  020 7923 1870 www.thetearooms.org
  Open: 11AM-6PM Mon to Fri,
  11AM to 6.30PM Sat and Sun
  Rail: Stoke Newington

Tina, We Salute You
  47 King Henry's Walk, Dalston N1 4NH
  020 3119 0047 www.tinawesaluteyou.com
  Open: 8am-5pm Mon, 8AM-7PM Tues to Fri,
  10AM-7PM Sat and Sun
  Tube/rail: Dalston Junction,
  Dalston Kingsland

Tinto Coffee
  411 Fulham Palace Road, Fulham SW6 6SX
  020 7731 8232 www.tintocoffee.com
  Open: 7AM-9PM Mon to Sun
  Tube/rail: Putney Bridge, Parson's Green

Yumchaa
  35 Parkway, Camden NW1 7PN
  020 7209 9641 www.yumchaa.co.uk
  Open: 8AM-8PM Mon to Fri,
  9AM-8PM Sat and Sun
  Tube: Camden Town, Mornington Crescent

IN MEMORY OF JULIANA SPEAR